CLOSE YOUR EYES, VISIONS

CLOSE YOUR EYES, VISIONS

MICHAEL RUBY

Station Hill Press

Barrytown, NY

Land Acknowledgment

In the spirit of truth and equity, it is with gratitude and humility that we acknowledge that the Institute for Publishing Arts, Inc., and Station Hill Press reside on the sacred homelands of the Munsee and Muhheaconneok people, who are the original stewards of this land. Today, due to forced removal, the community resides in Northeast Wisconsin and is known as the Stockbridge-Munsee Community. We honor and pay respect to them, as well as to their ancestors and future generations, and we recognize their continuing presence in their homelands. We understand that our acknowledgment requires us to recognize our own place in and responsibilities toward addressing inequity, and that this ongoing and challenging work requires that we commit to real engagement with the Munsee and Mohican communities to build an inclusive and equitable space for all.

Published by Station Hill Press, the publishing project of the Institute for Publishing Arts, Inc., 120 Station Hill Road, Barrytown, NY 12507, a not-for-profit, tax-exempt organization [501(c)(3)].

Online catalogue: www.stationhill.org
e-mail: publishers@stationhill.org

Cover and interior design by Stacy Wakefield Forte
Cover photography by Santeri Viinamäki/wikimedia commons

Library of Congress Cataloging-in-Publication Data
Names: Ruby, Michael (Michael Handler), author.
Title: Close your eyes, visions / Michael Ruby.
Description: Barrytown, NY : Station Hill Press, [2023]
Identifiers: LCCN 2022037714 | ISBN 9781581772203 (paperback)
Subjects: LCGFT: Poetry.
Classification: LCC PS3618.U325 C56 2023 | DDC 811/.6--dc23/
eng/20220912
LC record available at https://lccn.loc.gov/2022037714

Manufactured in the United States of America.

CLOSE YOUR EYES

VISIONS

For Henri Michaux

CLOSE YOUR EYES

When I finished graduate school at Brown University in June 1983, my youth of studying poetry and writing poetry was over. It was time for me to move out of the apartment in Providence where I'd just translated Andre Breton's "Cinque Rêves," where I'd learned a few months earlier how to transcribe the inner voices I heard as I was falling asleep. It was time to return home to the New York area after 8 years away and figure out some kind of career in publishing or journalism. Dreading the prospect, I took "a last summer off."

One afternoon in early June, my friend Owen Andrews picked me up at my father's apartment in South Orange, N.J., and we set off for his cabin outside Charlottesville. That night, we stopped at his friend Tal Mack's house in Middleburg, Va., where we slept in sleeping bags in a horse trailer that was open in the back. I hadn't slept much in several days—what with graduation and moving home to New Jersey. When I closed my eyes in the horse trailer, I immediately started seeing a vision. It was like watching a movie. That had never happened to me except when I was 13 and accidentally took 8 hits of acid at Jeffrey Pownes' house in South Orange.

Ever since that night in the horse trailer, whenever I haven't slept much for several days, I've been prone to these movie-like visions before sleep. They usually follow a similar script: I'm riding in a car, looking out the window at a 1960s suburban street, watching the houses and trees go by. I think of them as little movie clips that have survived in my brain from all those times I rode around town with my mother doing errands for a household of 10, before she went to work as a social worker at the Essex County Welfare Board in Newark and I started school.

Later in that June visit to Charlottesville, I became interested in another kind of vision, one that is familiar to many people, especially when they're listening to music. What do we see, this second, if we close our eyes? Colors. Shapes. Occasional images. In a poem commemorating the visit to Virginia, "I Chose to Remember," I wrote this line:

> I chose to remember I lay on the carpet with my eyes closed and saw a blue square, three green squares and a red circle.

This brief vision could be a Suprematist painting by Malevich from Moscow in the 1910s. It's like paintings by some of my favorite artists: Kupka, Kandinsky, Mondrian, Reinhardt, Newman, Rothko. It's part of a world of ever-changing colors and shapes, an abstract movie playing continuously in our brains just below the surface of consciousness, almost never perceived. Surely, these visions are a source of abstract visual art, just as dreams are a source of fiction and inner voices are a source of poetic lines.

For 20 years after that visit, I always had a vague idea of writing about this familiar human experience. In the meantime, I started to chronicle the dreams and fleeting memories and inner voices that are equally creations of our brains. In the early 2000s, after finishing the trilogy *Memories, Dreams and Inner Voices*, I finally returned to what we see with our eyes closed. At first, I wrote down what I saw in a notebook, but I found it taxing to keep opening my eyes to write, and it degraded my ability to see with my eyes closed. After a few sessions, I started wearing a blue airline eye mask and dictating into a recorder. That arrangement became the subject of frequent raillery from my three young daughters, proof that "Daddy's insane." This is what I saw when I repeated the mantra *Close your eyes*.

1

Close your eyes. There's a silver net in front of a black world.   Purple flowers grow in the black.   A horizontal bar of light crosses the black.

Silver stalks grow out of the black earth. Light. Just light. A flower of light in the very middle of the black.

Thin silver waterfalls spill   over a black cliff. Light bleeds out of sight to the left.   The sun shines down through an orange mist.

Silver leaves rise   in a slow fountain. Many silver planets twinkle. Purple flowers   rise out of sight. A silver tree soars down, then up. Black bats scatter the silver.

Green lily pads with pale yellow flowers cover the surface. Something blinding   from above.   A silver horizontal bar rises, pulsing. Something blinding.

The sun, at the other end of a valley, shines in my eyes.

2

The world is gold   afternoon sunlight on the ocean.

                                        Flakes of light fall like snow. It's
snowing flakes of light. The flakes   slow.
The lightfall lightens.

3

A gold mist descends. The left hemisphere is   gold, burnished gold.
The right is silver, running silver, dripping silver. A white vertical line divides
them. A flickering line. A silver gong trembles soundlessly high up on the
right. The spiky white light of bombs invades our upper world from below.
        This brown is so comforting, soporific. Relax.   There's a tiny
control panel, deep in all this darkness. One skunk stripe across the darkness.
A few brown ducks float in the silver water. The sun's deep in the water. And
what if the world becomes yellow, a muddy yellow, with a silver streak,
        and a tiny black horse's head? And what if it becomes a small silver
wheel turning? At the edge of the darkness,   there's a silver frost.   A
silver smudge,   like   when clouds cover the moon, and
you can't see the outline of the moon,   just some   light.

4

An orange mountain grows in the middle of this red world. The mast of a sailboat rises against the orange sunset. Yellow invades the orange from above
　　　　　and is repelled. A whiter light shines from the top of the world.
Bright yellow wings. (There is a storm in the world, wind blowing the grasses, grasses we'll never see, because we could become sick in them.)

This silver, this muddy silver. Red muddies silver. The red wears away
　　　into orange.
The sun is beyond.　　It's dangerous to look at the sun with your eyes closed.
Pure orange, beyond description.　A black pyramid.　A purple pyramid dissolves in the orange. It turns into a hat. A fat yellow arrow points upward to the right, rises out of sight.　Clouds of orange.

Pale yellow, the yellow of chickens, with blood vessels showing right below the skin.
And now, a lime-green flower blooms. It turns yellow.
　　　　And now, the purple triangle turns into a church, becomes misty, blistered, like one of Monet's paintings of Rouen cathedral. It enlarges.

A purple dog looks down at me, disappears.

Two specks, not obviously a pair, float in the orange water, the sea of fire.
　　　　　　　The orange rose is a fireball.　The orange fireball is a
rose.

5

The world is white. The world is maroon, with a single black speck in the middle. The world is white. The world is maroon, with a pair of black specks falling. The world is white. The world is maroon, with black specks falling. The world is white. The world is maroon. There must be something beyond this.

The world is black, pulsing.

The world becomes so very calm at these moments. A mysterious breeze.
    The world is bright red. Are those shadows, faint black shadows? The world is brown. Yellow invades   from the upper right.

The world is white. The world is maroon. Two black specks fall, loop to the left. Three black specks, a triangle, fall out of sight.

6

A silver net hangs   on a black wall, the threads   so thin.   A burst of
rainbow colors beyond? The world is warm.

       Very warm. The world draws sweat out of us.   A propeller
starting, a monoplane at an airfield. The ace. The tomboy. The tomcat.
What's a tomcat? The world is too warm.

The world is a mess. A weird silver-blue light is   emitted from the middle
of the mess, jagged flashes. A face, or scene, is about to emerge but
doesn't. The world is confused, everything in motion, I can't tell what
anything is. A white pyramid of light descends from above. It becomes a
white mist, it floats down, it settles on the ground and disperses.

The   silver net hangs   on a black wall, brightening in some parts,
dimming in others, never very bright. There's light.

       It brightens and dims, like the moon behind changing cloud cover.

7

The world is white. A white rain.   A white box. Pulsing.
    Splattering on me.

The world is black. Seen through a white mist. There might be a white face.
Clownish. Garish. Black invades from below and quickly blots everything
out.

Silver. For an instant. Dizzyness.

Brown. Milky brown. Light invades from above. White plants grow tall.

Jet black. Through a red mist.   An orange mist never takes over. A
white blur in the black   shrinks and disappears. A thin silver geyser sprays
into the black.   This oval is black. Raindrops hit the black water.

A silver crescent,   the letter C. A form with a thick inky outline. A white
mountain range. A puff of white smoke above a house.

A chalky black. Snow drifting down.

Something so red in the black.   Through a yellow mist.

8

Close your eyes. The world is red, white and blue.   Sparkling silver.

A gold rain falls during the night. A gold rain falls the next night. A gold mist.
An orange light lights up the beach at night.

The world is yellow. Almost too bright. Fat bubbles, fat bubbles of mercury,
float upward.

9

The world is sparkling gold. There's a black cow. A huge black cow.

Gold drizzles down the black window. A gold aura enters from above, pulsing. A yellow river flows across the black earth, from right to left. Call it light. Call it electricity.

The sun rules,   yellow and deep brown. Deep, deep brown.

A cloud the shape of a flag. A black crossbow. A sun rising from below ground. It falters. Slips back. A black queen sits on a gold throne. A wispy three-dimensional triangle. Solids made of spiderwebs, like Pevsner or Gabo sculptures. Small white figures, jerky, like   an early movie. A white arched window, high up on the right.

An X-ray of a woman wearing a bridal veil. Do people and cats turn white when they're electrocuted? The black waves rise, they rise and rise, making me feel queasy.

The world is orange and black, dense orange and black dots, with something whipping through them, wind or water or an invisible animal.

The world is a dark wood. Sparse grass grows in the black world. It ripples.

A train window at night reflects   bottle-green light.

A fountain at night in a lurid light.

A white rectangle blinks, high up on the right.   It's instantly blotted out by black.   Then   an amorphous shape,   inkier, disturbing. It trembles, the vague outlines shifting.

10

The world is pink lemonade swaying. Swaying like ocean water.

Something yellow fails to take shape. Red. A red skirt. Rustling. In the wind.
Folds of gray animal skin. Her yellows and browns were   best. Yellow.
    Lemon yellow. Lemon.

11

The world is a fire. A fire has   shadows. They grow.   A   question mark falls through this fire, falls through this orangeade. God drinks this orangeade, I'm   sure of it. Three black dots,   a triangle, drift down and settle on the bottom. The pale orange is the beginning of the world. A blue truck floats out of the orange.

Vanilla custard is yellow like this. This health never reaches us. Nothing reaches us.   The orange world is spattered with red. Yellow decorates. Yellow stabilizes.

Beyond the yellow mist,   a faint purple. Light breaks everything and reassembles it as orange clouds with red outlines.   An orange ladder descends into our hearts. The ladder turns molten. From the yellow mist, a purple mist rises.   Orange pudding. What is orange pudding? I know   I've eaten it.

12

The world is orange, with dark fuzzy edges. The fuzziness takes over. The
world is brown. Black hawks fly up to it. A black cloud hangs over it. A
musical note floats upward.   The world is yellow, blinding. There are
four or five tiny bubbles on the edges of this yellow,   this yellow
     quickly passing through orange into brown. A dot falls   like a worn-
out balloon. A dot falls and   curves to the left, turns upward.
          In the bright brownness, or the brown brightness.

Two black dots sit at the top of a burning world. Something hangs down from
each of them, like a string from a balloon.   The balloons   keep floating up
and up, but never out of sight, as if   bouncing against an invisible ceiling.
Things are surprisingly static, an occasional bright thing, dark thing, but the
overall color   orange or a   maroonish brown.
          For a moment   a yellow barge, a   fat thing poking into the
world from below. But it's so transient, muddying, not clarifying.

The world is yellow, bright yellow. Suddenly blood red. A sort of textured red,
with orange seeping through from behind.   One black dot trembles in the
middle near the top.   There's another,   larger, just above it.
They tremble and rise. Now there's just one, still rising, still rising.   A
wind blows it into two dots. Rising like the tips of flames,   flying into the
upper atmosphere. The world is a cooler yellow, with gray behind,   and one
dot,   maroon, stuck in the far left, stuck as the yellow turns to silver.

          A starry night, a dim globe of light in the black.   Glowing white fish
swim through the darkness.

The world is orange. A frightening orange. Black dots bounce like ping-pong
balls against the ceiling. The brightness   invades from there.

The world is yellow, pale yellow, but threatening to flip to maroon, or lavender. Lavender seeps through the yellow, little clouds of lavender. Black dots bounce away in every direction. A mist of lavender converges in the middle.

A single black dot rises speedily   then suddenly curves down and disappears to the left   as if that were its plan.

Beyond yellow is yellow white. A flowery color. In the end, there are two black dots, one at the top and one at the bottom. In this maroon liquid. There's one black dot, on the right,   bouncing off the bottom.

13

Close your eyes.   Two black dots cling to each other. The more the world trembles, the more they cling. The world turns the color of butter.

                    The orange world is spattered with bright red. Bright red powder.
          Yellow feathers. Yellow scales. They pale.

14

A sheer silver fabric hangs   in front of a black world.

The world is a giant rose, a black rose with silver edges on its infinite petals.

The black world has faint silver trails that seem to join up with each other but don't lead anywhere, just round and round.

The black is dissolving. The world turns salt and pepper, a most unappetizing pale gray salt.

A pulsing   silver bar blocks my   vision. The criminal remains anonymous, the detainee   anonymous. The bar dissolves,
            back into black.

15

The world is a silver mist, and beyond   black.

The world is a yellow mist, and beyond   a silver mist, and beyond   black.

The world is a silver mountain, against a black sky. A silver smile. A silver valley, with silver slopes. A silver man carrying a pack.

The world is a starry night, so many stars, stars and stars and stars and stars.

The world is lit   by radiation.   Half lit. A quarter lit. A sixteenth lit.

The world is a black shadow on a silver screen. What is the world the shadow of? What is the shadow of?

There are gray windows in the lower right.   A thin gray window in the center.

Confetti lands softly.

    Near a harbor.

The world is black, with a tiny green pattern across the whole surface. I can't make it out.

16

The world is a silver mist. A small ball spins in the middle.

It's morning, or   it's going to be morning.

                              There's a lime-green corridor
into the depths of darkness. A narrow corridor.

There's a fire on the water at night.   A very pretty fire
on the water.

The world glitters like Liberace's jacket.

All sorts of purples and blue-grays. I can't tell what's being depicted. There's
a purple turtle in the middle of the darkness.

Uh oh,   a tiny sun is being born, shining, blowing up.

The turquoise trails of invisible objects.

The world has a black whirlpool in the middle. Who can say where it leads?

This question mark.

This minutely tattooed white column. Tilted a little to the left.

17

A silver mist floats in front of a black world. A black bird towers over me. Two silver rivers flow together in the middle.

The silver sun, with delicate threadlike rays, shines down from the left.   The world sways like ocean water. Something struggles to emerge from the silver threads.

An orange stain. An orange stain looks like a continent on the black water. A black tree leaps up,   the shape of a pitchfork. Africa is outlined in gold leaf. Two brown ducks on a black pond. A star flaring up at the bottom.
         A buttocks and thigh.

The world is profoundly dark. But as always, you begin to make out things. There's a steep rise, a butte. How will the horsemen ever get up there? Wave after wave of black,   each inkier than the last,   nauseates me. A star flames out at the bottom of the world, drowning in the black water.

The black   bids us to sit down.   There's a comfortable white seat made from spiderwebs.   White spiderwebs. The material's so strong it could hold up a black hole.   In fact, it does. Two black holes. Just sitting around.   The world is a curtain of water, a waterfall, with a black cave behind it. Let's try to reach that cave. Is there a green   in there?   A head?   A peach pit? And if there's a peach pit,   shreds of peach?

Instead of a black bird, a gold pyramid stands over me.   The gold shines through black clouds straight into my eyes. The gold sun—it's gonna do something for me, it's gonna take me somewhere.   A train hurtles across a narrow gorge.   A train hurtles above a threadlike waterfall.
         A Hawaiian waterfall.

   The windows of the upper storey are brown. Black butterflies with lime outlines fill the sky, collide with each other. Gold shapes, puzzle pieces, float away. The road begins gold, but   soon   blackens. Soon we don't know where the road is.   There's a glowing, pinkish-white boulder along   the road.   A skyline of sorts, a translucent skyline. The gold light shone on her and turned her into a chicken.   The silhouettes of people talking.

18

The world is silver, trembling. A steep black mountain rises up. This mountain won't help us. The world is muddy.   Mud. Featureless.

The world is smooth today.   Uniform.

Somewhere, there is light. But it doesn't make much headway here.

The world is featureless. It gives us nothing.
                    Nothing to talk about.
          Nothing to see today. Perhaps that's the point.

But wait, are those bushes at the edge of the darkness? Radiating their shape, their curved tops? I guess not. Once again,   the sense of light coming from above. But it doesn't illuminate anything.   Not a single object. It just seeps into the darkness.

    The world is a silver mist with lines cutting through it,   a spiderweb at night.

Sometimes, the world reminds me of a spiderweb, and we are flies caught in it. Not knowing we're caught   until we can't deceive ourselves any longer.

Smoke rises at night,   listlessly. The fire died down a long time ago.

I sense trees in the darkness, with white flowers. Small trees in the darkness with white flowers.

The world is frosted,   frost covering a window. The world is the color of dust. The world is dust. In the middle of this charcoal world,   a black dot grows and shrinks,
      grows and shrinks. It looks like an ink blot.

19

The world is orange. There's a black dot in the orange, falling, falling to the bottom. It bounces on the bottom, a low bounce.   Two   more black dots. They don't fall. They drift down and then leap up, drift down and   leap up, all the while staying at   the same height. The third ball at the bottom does the same.

Now the three balls at different levels fall and   bounce, fall and   bounce. Everything we see is falling and   bouncing. The world continuously falls and   bounces, falls and   bounces.

The world is orange. A black dot drops like a stone.

The world is watermelon red, with a   slightly shapeless rectangle in the middle,   dusty brown. It's gone now. Only   watermelon red. There's one black dot, which bounces close to the top, close to the very top. It's gone, flown away.

Now the world is the most inviting creamy orange, the orange of a creamsicle, my mother's favorite Good Humor. And there are two black dots, one at the top and one in the middle, and they seem to be connected by the thinnest black thread.

20

The world is black,   with yellow radiating   from the upper left. The
world is black, with many yellow threads hanging down.   A few yellow
threads run crosswise. Surely, the yellow threads are going to become
something. They're going to grow into something. They swell into bushes, tall
hedges. The yellow will make something of itself. But this silver, this silver,
soon gives way to gold flashes on black water. There's a vague silver object in
the middle of the water.

The world is black. Silvery black. Muddy black.   Two club-like objects
at the top.   Bright yellow, with orange edges. There's a black object
in the middle of the orange world,   a torso. Brown mold eats it away. The
world is charcoal gray. A maroon object,   a profile, tries to emerge in the
upper left, but it never does,   and slowly drifts out of sight, very slowly.
The charcoal gray turns, in slow increments,   lime green. There's a V-
shaped turquoise in the middle of the black,   a turquoise vase.

21

The world is yellow, custard yellow, very alluring. There are   some black dots around. They stay at the top and bottom. The yellow is turning to orange juice. Lemon juice and orange juice. There is something black or purple—yes, purple—that tries to emerge, but it doesn't try very hard, and it doesn't emerge.

The world is bright orange, royal orange.   There's a black dot in the center, and a small teardrop nearby. And both are drifting to the right. The world is blue and green. They're drifting into   light green. The dot moves around in the center, but that's all, it's not going anywhere. It never goes far.

The world is this white yellow, this eggnog yellow. There's a round purple object with jagged edges at the top of the yellow. It's out of sight. The yellow turns to watermelon, then back toward yellow.
          This is not what I wanted, but it too is good. This is yellow, with a trace of black mixed into it. There's a black ball high up on the right that wants to go somewhere, that wants to slash toward the center,
               but it can't, it's restrained by invisible ties.

This world is white, a   dark white. Is that possible? Is black mixing into this white? Is maroon? Is orange?

22

The world is yellow, gold, orange, blinding. Two black dots are swept along
from left to right, fade out. Yellow stripes the orange. There's something
out of control on the left, a pulsing vertical object. It seems to have a yellow
and blue aura. A pulsing   candlestick. And now orange, fringed in
black and white, lies   on top of me.   There's a black dot
below the middle.   Everything turns black. Everything turns orange.
Crimson. There are four or five black dots. They like to lurk along the edges.
Everything turns black.

The world is white.   The world is
lemon meringue. And that's how it stays, for a long time. Still this beautiful
lemon white, the lemon white of certain roses, certain ice cream,   certain
light.

There's a black dot in the middle of the orange, orangeade orange.
The orange turns to brown, which turns to blue, and   a black dot   floats
at the very bottom.

The world is half bright red and half dull black, a right half and a left half, a
jigsaw-puzzle border between them. Now it's yellow on the left and black on
the right. And soon it's all muddy brown, orange showing through, a black dot
rising with the flames, rising, rising, getting smaller, still in view, still in view,
drifting to the right.

The world is yellow, with a black dot in the middle, falling.   Not falling
out of view. Lingering just above the bottom. Sometimes bouncing up,   a
little. Being pushed up by a   kind of hair along the bottom. An eyelash?

   The world is purple with a big yellow hole in the middle.   The world is
raining blue, raining green, yellow.   A black dot in the middle drops   to
the bottom.   The world is purple with an orange object in the middle. It's all
orange now. Orange shading   into yellow.

The world turns crimson, blood red. Brown rises from below, purple-tinged brown, taking over everything.   There's a black dot in the lower left, where the *green* appears, and now the *green*, with some blue, pushes through everything, and now light blue pushes through.

The world is olive green, with a yellow vertical bar on the right, a yellow horizontal bar on the bottom.   Bright orange, blood orange, with two dots moving   frenetically high up on the right. Real jumping jacks.

The left half is maroon and the right half   orange. They're divided by a vertical line,   a fuzzy area between the two colors. This is what Rothko painted, isn't it? This is the surface of the sun, things bubbling out,   leaping out.   That's what we see, the surface of the sun.

23

The world is gold, blinding. It feels like something might come out of the middle, but nothing does. There are   four black dots in the orange. One of them has

a long hair trailing from it. The dots don't move much. The orange turns to gold. The dots leap up. Now there are three dots. They don't

move much. Quietly, the world turns yellow, tapioca, very soft. There are a few black dots in the pudding.   But they're not very pronounced. The world is lemon yellow,   delectable. The world is candy-apple red, with a few flaws. A few dots trembling. The world turns

the color of punch. The color of certain apples. Of certain paintings. The upper half orange, the lower half red, with a black dot in the red, just below the dividing line. The world is custard yellow, but a mist of blood red seeps in

from below. Orange punch. Blood orange.   Bright orange, blinding orange, overpowering orange. A few dark smudges, especially in the middle. Smudges that want to be the footprints of tiny animals. A dark mass, a dark fog, purple fog, is rising up, rising up.   A mountain. The world is lemon yellow again. The left half is lemon yellow.   The right half   a cloudy purple. The purple engulfs everything. The world is yellow, a sweet yellow.

The world is pure yellow, not too bright, not sweet and inviting. With veins of pale blue.

24

The world is many overlapping silver window frames looking out on black.

The world is black. A silver mist forms on   the black
window. A sketchy silver horse rides toward us. A silver flower opening.
Silver hair spreads out in the water. The silver will be silver in this shadowy
room   on a gloomy afternoon. I   see a person I once knew.   Flaring
    nostrils.   Someone from Little League.

The world is mostly black.   Black granite
with tiny red pockmarks, static on the surface. The side of the world is made
of black granite. Nothing is carved on it. It's smooth now. Nothing emerges
from it. If anything, it must be approached. It doesn't approach. In the gloom,
I perceive a tree that was chopped down,   shoots coming out of the stump.
      Energetic. You can hardly see the stump anymore.   On the other
side of this black water, there's a bright light. The water blackens.
There's an area of pure black, which enlarges and   shrinks, enlarges and
shrinks. But, if anything, it's shrinking overall. Far out in that black,
      somewhere far out in that black,   across a prairie, there are fireworks.
This blue being, this purple being, flies around the landscape. Is it Krishna?
It's taken a long time for this blue-gray being to emerge.

The world is still black and gray, or black and silver. It's been that way the
whole time.   So uninteresting.
      Black   with   silver swirls, silver mist.

Now there's a   silver burst in the lower part of the world. Where are those
balloons and balls falling? What happened to them?

25

The world is black, with orange sparkles. A   black sky filled with stars. A depth of stars.   A trembling circle in the middle. And larger concentric circles radiating out from it.

The world is black. Blacker and blacker in the center. Horizontal lines of charcoal   barely distinguishable. Black is best, pure black, but it's hardly possible.

The world is black. Raked by light from above on the right, and then the left.

The world is black, with a vague   mask floating
        along the bottom. A large clump of dust. A large mud stain. A cloudiness in the bottom of a glass. A cloudiness billowing upward, muddying the world.

The world is black, with sunny billows floating up and away.
Billows with orange auras.

26

The world is gold, gold   sparkling on a black or red background. Gold
sparkling on a black background, which is itself on a black background.

The world is orange, with a precipice at   the top. A black precipice.
Black water arching down. A black cataract.

Each constellation of small stars is a different insect, creeping along the
ground, the yellow ground.

27

Gold alps stand against a black sky, trembling.
      The gold letters are unreadable, breaking up against the black,
    turning into gold mist. A dark green garment hangs down, black in the
middle. A dark gray garment hangs down, black in the middle.

28

The world is starry,   a cloud of stars, a mist of stars.

The world trends toward black, but with orange bursts. Geysers of fire.

        The world is black, with the shadow of a guitar player. The big
guitar slanting   across the middle.

The world is dark, with   a couple of vertical stripes, like an Ad
Reinhardt painting. Light leaks into this dark world from several places. Light
leaks in, and joins to form a mist. Light is. Light isn't.   Light is.

29

Close your eyes.   The world is gold, flashing.
         Fish scales in the sun. The world is not beginning. The world is
yellow. The world is the inside of a mango. The world is no place we've ever
been, except during lovemaking. The world is no place we've ever been.

The world is black, covered with this yellow   static. Light shines down on
the black   from the   right. As it crosses   down to the left, it
warps. The light is warping, right   there. And then over there, the light
warps.   The world is a dark
alley through   trees, an increasingly dark alley. We never reach the end of it,
because it leads into the past, into a place in a painting   150 years ago.

The world is yellow, very warm, very inviting, not intense. A soft yellow,
maybe a powdery yellow and black. A spiderweb should look like this. A
spiderweb could look like this. A spiderweb at the right time.

The world is going to be black now, at least for a moment. Before the giant
letters of billboards. Before the raccoon face, the panda face, emerging like a
rose from the muddy purple-gray-black background. Light shines into this
world. I'm not sure from where. Light falls on me, in several ways.
         Light falls across light.   Light falls on me. Light does fall.
Light is cheerful. Light is pastel. Light falls on a golf course, tennis courts, a
pool, a clubhouse, a dining room, the lunch specialties. Light is lurid, as in
early Giulio Romano. Light   brings out only the most iridescent colors in the
darkness.

The world is black, with a dab of custard yellow, like a custard yellow sweater
hanging over a chair, at the very bottom. A yellow translucent fish, a ghost
fish, feeding at the bottom.

The world is a blizzard at night. So much white powder, white powder as fine
as sugar or salt, falling out of the dark blue. Powder, arching over us.

The world is tired. Black and white going in different directions. The salt-and-pepper world is tired. This gray pudding won't be eaten today.

The world is alternately blinding and not. The surface has the texture of a huge white oak. The world is the sun shining on tree bark. The surface of the world is tree bark.

The world is black with silver dots.   The world is covered with silver powder. A black shape, indistinct beyond the gray powder. The black shape a horse jumping. In the middle of the black,   with faint silver highlights, a bear's head, a werewolf's head, a cat's head.

30

The world is black. The letter H, a large gold letter H, trembles.

        A silver sun tries to break through.

Within every black, there's silver, threads of silver, curlicues of silver. Blue clouds float at different levels in the black sky, in the black sky below us.

The world is black, a droopy   light shining through it. A coppery, droopy light.

We are, each of us, living in this unreal world. Is this true darkness now? Almost. There are   impossible-to-follow blue trails, squiggles, I don't know what, within the black.

A picture   can take your breath away. The eyes.

31

The world is black, with bewitching blue sparkles. Acrobats swirl through that mist. A white mountaineer   ascends   in the upper right.

The world is green and purple and silver and black, and maroon, and maybe the light of a train is entering.

The world is   sparkling silver, rustling silver, silver shading on the right into black, which spreads and takes over. But no, the silver holds its own below. Intensifies into white as its space narrows. And now, it is pushed out of sight. The world is all black, muddy black,   gray black.

The world is a tunnel of overarching trees, a   sunlit   hillside in the distance.

The world is sparkling silver, silver and black. A silver web across   black skyscrapers against a blue-black sky. A black, tattered spiderweb against the blue-black sky. The web seems alive. Maybe it's   the reflection of a web in moving water. The blue-black sky seems to push it away, parting it.   Or something else is parting it.

Silver bubbles float up from a purple-black world, white bubbles.

The world is coal-black with a green   gray web ... I don't know ... tattered cloth ...   hanging down.   Things lighten.   There are these molten silver objects. Birds, beings, cracked   beings, reflected in water.

The sun striping a mountain pool.

The world is a pale orange square. A pale orange square at the top of the world, in the middle, disappearing. Now there's this black depth, with green static.   This is where worlds are born,

or where they're not quite born,   they don't rise to that. And so, a
milky white engulfs everything, and black tries to engulf that, and the white
curdles into little bits of milk in the black liquid of the world.

The world is a young white oak, reaching out to me with many arms, in a
dusky wood.
                                                 There are these columns of
light, columns of light coming down into the wood, very thin,
                                 filaments. It's like living under a giant
jellyfish or man o' war.

The world is a shining yellow, a blinding yellow, yellow turning gold, turning
dusky. Brown sprinkled with yellow dust. The yellow of static.
        Yellow sparklers landing on white picnic blankets.

We have a black night in front of us. And around us. And above us. But not
below us. Below us,   more picnic blankets on the grass, more people
sitting,   and a dark mass of trees at the bottom, before
the street, and the creek, and the ballfields.

The world has the perfect amount of chrome catching the streetlights.
                        Illuminating the street corner. The little traffic
circle.

The world is a   crystal globe, a crystal chandelier, like in
an old-fashioned catering hall. O those places were nice, they had nice
desserts, they had cream pies.
You could almost eat the chairs,   the columns, the wallpaper. The
whole place was meant to be eaten.

32

The world is sunlit. The sun　　　floods down from the right.
A cranberry orange.

The world looks like fruit punch, dark around the edges. The sky is the color
of fruit punch. That would make most people happy.

The world is a multicolored cat's face, pointillist. A painting by Klee?

　　Horse-drawn carts cross　　　a field.

The world is big blue bat, a big blue bird.

The world is a blue-black outline, frightening. Batman. Against a green sun,
in an olive-green sky.

33

The world is black, with   yellow shadows, yellow mists, in the upper right.

Light struggles to enter this world.   It
can't make inroads. Light rolls off,   runs off,   runs down our black world,
shaken off the way water is shaken off   animals.

Light blooms on the black world, without changing it.

The world is orange-tinted, raspberry-tinted, a black mountain with a raspberry
top. A black mountain   and raspberry-colored waves radiating
from behind the mountain.   A raspberry sun behind the top of a black
mountain.

The world is black, with a bright white amoeba in the upper right.   It blurs,
fades out,   there's no trace of it.

There are traces of light in the black, shadows of light that blow across the
black, thin clouds of light rising   in the black. White smoke rises slowly up
the black sky. White smoke, from many sources along the ground. The smoke
that keeps rising, days after a bombing.

35

Silver static trembles in front of a black world. There's a large yellow   N
tilting to the right. It looks like a burning, toppling building. The world is two
silver potbellies pushing up against each other.

The world is black, with gold static dancing on top.   A light tries to shine
through, from behind. And mostly fails. The world is the black that contains
the loveliest blues. What is that? Teal blue? No, it's deeper than that.

The world is light gray. A light is trying to shine through.   Various greens—
snot greens—proliferate. The world is black, with various light greens lurking
within.   Winning greens.

36

The world is black, with blue glitter. It stays like that, black with blue glitter. And because the blue glitters, there is yellow. And because there is black, there is red, or at least a sense of red.

The world is tired. If not the world, I am tired. Light leaks in from below the world. Light leaks into the bottom of the world.

The world is black, with a large tan image, or shadow, flickering in its depths.

The world is black, with green and yellow and blue sparkles, rainbow sparkles, rising   to the right. Like the shadows of flames.

The world is yellow. Crisscrossed by food fights. With odd depths.
The world has more dimensions than usual.

The world is black, with a small circle bathed in yellow near the middle, yellow and black brushstrokes. A black object in the lower half of the world is surrounded by a squiggly blue aura, perhaps several auras. The world is black and yellow.

The world is black with yellow glitter blowing across.
            The light is not the surface of the sun. It's ambient light.
            Stray light.   Much-bounced light. It's been around. It's
bounced around.   It's the
light and shade, the fire and shadow,   that give the appearance
of life to inanimate things. The eye bounces between bright flame and dark
shadow, and things seem to move.

37

A blue mist floats in front of a black world.   A mist of faint stars.

The blue mist   doesn't change much. Occasionally   milkier. But nothing emerges from it. A gray cloud seems to form in the middle. But becomes nothing.

The black,   the blue mist, make me sleepy. The blue mist becomes a mist of light. There's a bright dot high up on the right.   Briefly.

Light invades the black world from below. There are bursts of light, bursts of blue light.

The world is black, with a fire burning in the middle, in the distance. The world is black, with a gold clash in the middle. A "clash of civilizations"? A gold mist floats in front of a black world. Overlapping panes of gold mist. The world is black, with a pallid amoeba in the middle. It dissolves. The world is black, with a succession of explosions in the middle. The world is made of gold foil rippling in breezes.

A beautiful purple light takes over the black. A purple that doesn't exist in nature, except maybe a few flowers. There's a bright star in the middle of the purple that gets brighter and brighter without enlarging, and then dissolves.

The world is black, behind a blue mist,   pulsing,   trembling.

38

A silver mist floats in front of a black world.   So black. A
thicker silver mist   radiates outward from this black center. The black
world beyond.   Pure black.
                                Maybe   the color of molasses. It has some
depth. Some brown.   But black has more depth than brown, doesn't it?
Lemon yellow swirls into the black,   but   remains an   arch high
up on the left.

The world is yellow and brown. A big ship moving away from me. A lion—or
a tiger—just standing in the sun.   This yolky area at the top of the world.
It   glistens, surrounded by gray, gray and black mist, smoldering or
flashing like some paintings by Rembrandt.   Lurid.   Not lurid.
                The luridness of gold.   Gold cloth. Gold
brocade.

The world is black, with a yellow tree. With a yellow dance. With a yellow
sun. Trying to burn through   clouds. But never getting   far. A blinding
speck at most. And then, swallowed up, the way the moon gets swallowed up.
    You can tell where it is from the brightness of the clouds, and then the
  brightness becomes   dispersed, and you can no longer tell.

The world is black, with great depth.   Milky light seeps in from the left, and
soon covers   the entire world except   far down on the right.

        The world is black, but   not flat. The world is flat, but   not black.
The world is flat, and   black. The world is black, and   flat. Only the first
of those propositions is true at the moment.

The world is blue-black, with a yellow glow above and beyond the mountain
range.   The world is black, with a dark green hook, an artificial hand,
reaching out. The world is a television station, a   shopping strip, the upper
stories of a white suburban house in the sun. In the center of the black world is

a small, bright yellow face, with big, bright yellow lips, talking. I can't hear what it's saying   except that it's serious, and   mean, and demands attention. And then,   concentric circles, yellow rings, radiating outward from it. And then,   demonic faces, robotic faces, in a yellow wash, over   white paper. There are so many trees in this darkness, mature trees, and   underbrush mostly removed, the way it's supposed to be in a French forêt.

The world is black, with yellow   high up on the right. A large yellow man is wearing a brown coat, which he takes off. A bird head. A baby chicken's head, with brown feathers, black feathers. Neon radiates   out of a woman's eye, out of her left eye. Silver, and pink, and blue.
                                                 I'm seeing a vision now. It's like a movie—it's literally moving—of a landscape out West, pale blue sky,   a few clouds.   I'm seeing it out the window of a moving vehicle. It's   exactly like a movie,   for 10 seconds. Now, I'm not seeing it, it's all   dark.

39

Close your eyes. The world is black. Thickly sown with   dim stars.

                                                                    The world is
unchanging.   Light infiltrates
the darkness without   amounting to anything. Light muddies the darkness.
Nothing emerges. The light doesn't amount to much. A house at a crossroads
in the desert. The light doesn't amount to much. A   memory from 30
years ago of driving north on the Garden State Parkway at night, under the
Irvington Ave. and Springfield Ave. overpasses. The light doesn't amount to
much, except sleep.

40

An orange tree pulses   in the night. There's a crucifixion. The man's
dead. A plane's wing bursts into flames, not far above   ground.
          Looking across a river, at this dusky hour, I can almost see the
trees on the other side. And the telephone poles. And a galleon, reflected in
the river.
          The river becomes a lake,   with a mountain rising on
the other side. A yellow ladder arches   into a black hole, an animal's open
mouth. A frightened animal's open mouth. A dead animal's open mouth.

So many little fires burn. Burning candles cover the top of a table. Their
smoke becomes an orange cloud in the black.   There is a large
hole at the top of the world, and yellow smoke is billowing down into the
black.   The world is suddenly so much sunnier.
                    Sunlit green,   the sun on the edge of the
woods.

In the black night, cars drive toward me, with muffled headlights. Here's a
truck, with its headlights off. The cars and trucks are   coming out of a
tunnel. I feel sure they're going to steer to my right and avoid me. A car heads
toward me, on this foggy night, its headlights muffled. The   trees soak up
some of its light. The low leaves are incandescent orange.

Now,
          I'm under a wedding tent, at night, in   summer. A white trolley pulls
up. A woman gets out,   walks confidently in the sunlight across the tracks,
          bubbling.

High   in the gray darkness, there's a tiny, deep blue window, with a bright
yellow star at the top.   On top of the buildings, there are yellow
ladders, thin but sturdy. On   top of the houses,
          peaked roofs with slippery fish-scale shingles.   A large, pale

blue house, behind two big trees, its second floor   bigger than its first floor.
And now, I begin to fade. Even
though the world takes on the colors   of early Giulio Romano. Flame-
lit cliffs, fire-lit cliffs.   The light of a   fire reverberates off
the cliffs. The caves are ink. The cave mouths are black ink.

We are insects in our command of this space.   Dragonflies in our command
of space.   Birds in our command of space.
There's an orange and yellow bird, in the dark night.
Indeterminately lit.

The world is a curtain of stars. A curtain of light bubbles. Turquoise,
aquamarine bubbles, so minute, like an erotic sketch.

An animal sits   high up in a tree, where there's still   light left from the
sunset, a small animal, about the size of a head, a face. Yawning. Screaming.
Demonic. Sly. It looks like an archbishop's hat.
There's a slit   in the red, rocky hillside for
machine guns. The face of a tadpole, with eyes and mouth of light. The grass
blades are made of light. The spiderwebs are made of light.

A woman is talking in the middle of a large group of people on the shore.
Everyone listens   until her head turns into a horse's head, and all the other
heads turn into horses' heads, and then they fog out, like the people in
Bocchioni's "Stati d'animo."   This is one of the last places lit by the sun
today. The thoughtless light. Gray velvet touched by yellow light.
Decorated with pinpoints of light.
Leaves. Gold leaves. Burning leaves. Gold hands. Burning hands. The
flaming hands are never consumed, they never hurt. Her hands seem to be in
flames.

41

The world is black,   with bright red trying to pierce through   from behind, red spikes of light, like reflections on water at night.

The world is a mix   of yellow and brown, inviting.   Warmer than usual, warmer to us. Metal rings hang from a black wall. Nothing comes toward us. We feel ourselves narrow.   Our frame of reference narrow.   Our field of vision narrow.   Narrowed into a line that stretches far behind us.

They look   like people in a photo from 40 years ago, unreal.
                        Their exact faces are unreal. People actually are not like this anymore.

The world sways, dances. The shadow of all this light sways. Like an evergreen.

Flares in the night. Yellow, with a blue edge.

Pink flowers want to break through the black.   Break open. And they do. And they almost do. Pink. Soft. Peonies. Pink peonies.

The world is a reflecting pond at night. The pond has   grays. And thus,   whites.   Have you ever noticed at night how all the available light will sometimes collect on a single object? A single low flare lights up the ground. Like a sunlamp. Like the sunlamp my brother Stephen used on the third floor of our house 40 years ago. What of that still exists? Not my brother, not the sunlamp, not our family. Only the house.

Close your eyes. There's light.   Clouds of light. Each cloud made   of countless tiny balls of light. Sometimes the clouds of light surge at us. They stain us. They enhance our breathing.

The world is a night scene by Giulio Romano.

The world narrows us. Narrows us to the width of our nose. Narrows us into sheets

of steel plate.   The world turns into white icing, lemon icing,   whipped cream, spilling down. Spindrift, spilling down. Like a long white beard, spilling down.

The world is black and white, black and gold. Some people wear gold hats in the restaurant booths.

42

The world is black, releasing a silver mist. A mist of silver stars, none distinct, none pinpointable. A trace of blue, blue-black, burns through the middle. It doesn't lead anywhere.

Jagged mountain peaks at night. Depths on the right. I don't know what causes them. Grassy humps in the sun.

The sun invades, the sun breaks through the world's defenses. The light kindles certain leaves, certain branches. The light flows in through pipes. I can see it making a turn in a right-angle pipe.

43

The world is a yellow explosion, turning orange,   then red, as it radiates outward. One black dot floats, in the middle. A second black dot appears in the upper left, and flows out of sight. We don't know when this   is going to end.

The world whitens, but only so much, and then   blackens, but only so much. It reaches a muddy black, a greenish black, even a whitish black. The world whitens, but only so much, and then   blackens, but only so much. At the top of the world, sunlight reasserts itself. The sunlight is going to enter us. It stretches us out.   Lays us out to dry. To dry straight. To be easily transportable.

A capful of   lemon yellow has been poured into the liquid air. Enriched, the air turns the color of orange juice, warm orange juice.

The world is bright orange, pure orange, as orange as   can be. The sun is too bright now to continue.

44

The world is purple, or orange, or maybe purple with orange bleeding in from behind. There are three black dots, near the top. One falls to the bottom and disappears. The second one drifts down toward the middle. Somehow, the purple becomes an arch that opens into more purple. There are four dots—a triangle and one dot out on its own. There are many dots, but most important, a pair of dots in the middle, that move in tandem with my breathing, or blinking, or heartbeat. One dot near the top has a long tail, like a comma, or a spermatozoa. The end of the tail becomes hairlike. There's another one, with such a long tail, the tail is ten times as long as the dot. They're like tiny black balloons, with long strings, floating. What more do we need to see?

The world is lemon yellow, with a few black dots, spread-out dots. They don't move much. They rise up and down a little, with the breeze, or with my breathing. In the middle of this yellow world, there's a clot, a ball of yellow hair, a tangle of yellow hair. A flower wants to form in the center. Inside the yolk of a fertilized egg. One of the bouncing dots has grown a long hairlike tail again. It bounces, or bounds, at the bottom of the world. The yellow reddens, pinkens. There's a bright red hole in the center. The color of Hawaiian Punch, hard to take seriously.

45

There are countless stars against a black sky. The stars join up, forming a spiderweb, a net. It   stays like that. For some reason, it makes me think of scrambled eggs.   There's a shadowy narrative   I can't quite put my finger on, taking place in this trembling, starry sky. Like the scenes you can observe in the dark areas between flashes of moonlight on the ocean.
                                          The night is streaked with silver. Moving silver.

The world is black, with endless stars, a   film of stars, a dirty film of stars. Each star is a muddy snowflake. Each star is a gothic letter, too dim and   smudged to read.

The world is a sieve of light. Light sprinkles through a million holes. A million needles of light.   The world is dark gray, with lighter areas within,   where galaxies seem to come into existence or fly apart.   It's all very hard to say. It's all very hard to see. This part of the universe is not so illuminated. The world is almost black. But I know the light will never wholly disappear.

The world gives me nothing today. The world gives next to nothing.   A memory of a fruit and vegetable market on Putnam Avenue in Cambridge, on the walk home to 141 Western Avenue 30 years ago. That's what the world gives, next to nothing, a random happy moment. The world giveth.

The world is black, behind a faint cloud of light that tries to thicken, but doesn't   succeed, and so the light remains scattered, shattered,
                  translucent islands floating in the black.   That is perhaps the answer: Light is an island in darkness.
                  Light fractures into an infinite number of islands floating in darkness. Light floats in a black ocean. Light rises out of a black ocean.

The world is almost black. Light barely filters through,   and don't ask me how it filters through.   Light filters through everywhere, but so little light.   Light filters through everywhere, but so little light.

Why is there light at all? Why is there darkness?

There's a cloud of light in front of the black.   A film of light. Like a film of dust, lying on the black.   No colors tonight, just light and darkness, no colors at all, not one. Or perhaps   yellow and black. *The Yellow and the Black*, a novel.

46

The world is black. The world is black for now.

VISIONS

For five years, I dictated what I saw with my eyes closed, ever-changing visions of colors and shapes and occasional imagery. They could be scripts for mostly abstract movies, some as brief as 10 seconds, others as long as 10 minutes. At the beginning of the sixth summer of dictation, I made an accidental discovery: If I closed my eyes and focused on an area of turbulent light in the dark visual field, I was much more likely to see brief realistic and surrealistic visions. My mantra from then on became *Close your eyes and look for areas of turbulence in the visual field*. I think of these areas as burbling fountains of fragmentary visions that only reach consciousness under certain conditions, such as mental illness or surrealist research. They are another creation of our brains that we rarely or never remember, like the inner voices before sleep that occasionally accompany them. Sometimes, a brief vision will connect with a moment in my life, like waiting outside a candy store on Tremont Avenue in East Orange, N.J. But I've never been anywhere near a county airport runway at night. Eventually, I found out where my visions led.

▼

An old car slows down
and parks at a corner.
A man gets out
and enters a candy store
with a large window
with green wood trim
and a Breyers ice-cream sign.

This might be a vision
of a moment far in the past,
a place I only went
once or twice as a child,
on Tremont Avenue
in East Orange
a few blocks east
of the Veterans Hospital.

July 9, 2007

▼

I see a white flower
in the middle
of a black world.
It leaves behind
a faint mist.

Now I'm inside
an ornate church
in Stockholm, of all places.

There's a muddy hole
in the middle of the world.
I'm not sure
if I'm looking
down into the hole
or up
into the hole.
Reasonable people
can disagree
(as reasonable people say).

There's something to see,
I can feel it.

July 16, 2007

▼

It's the first moment of dawn.
We're not going to see anything here.
Some shoes and clothes
strewn on the floor.
Some glasses and plates
left on the table.
This plant
reminds me of a ladder.

The ticket office
is quiet.
A cup of coffee
cools on the zinc counter.

His car
is stored on blocks
in the shed.
A cloud
presses against
the sole small window.
A tire
hangs from a tree
outside.
An elephant
sits
under the tree.
The elephant
has never been so young.

On a flat embankment
above a river
denuded by the Army Corps of Engineers,
glasses glint in the grass.

A purple bottle
sits on the middle of the table.
No one comes
and sits at the table.
It's funny,
for some obscure reason.

Pink and purple flowers
line the edge of the garden.
A blonde girl
comes partway out the screen door,
stops for a second,
and returns to the kitchen.
Light
coats
a giant white fungus
on the side of a tree.

Purple waves
spread outward from the man's head
in the black room.
Purple sky
fills the deepest cranny in the valley,
turning it into a reservoir.

Look, a mountain
at the end of the night.
You can see it
if you lean
very close
to the aquamarine water.
The lake
has extra coves,
extra

crenellations
at night.
The lake water
is purple.
There's one light
across the lake.
A single light,
not a lit house.
I want to say
it's a red light.
But it isn't a red light.
It's a white light,
a light light.

The sky
comes down to us
tonight.
The sky
touches us.
The sky
gets between us.
A little bit of the sky
runs into a storm drain.
I don't know
where it goes from there.

You won't ever net
this pink flying fish.

He sees
the side of her leg
in the doorway,
her left thigh.
That's what he sees first.

Round tables
fill the rooms at a club
on slightly different levels.
He waits for his friend.
His friend and his friend's friends.
He waits for the waiter.
The waiter
waits
for his friend and his friend's friends.
The room quietly turns orange.
The fireplace has nothing to do with it.
The fireplace is fake.
A tendril
climbs the wall
and runs along the lattice ceiling.
Will it drop something down to them?

The sun rises over the far side of the lake.

Fossils
stick out of the brown mud
at the bottom of a pit.

Shafts of light
try to penetrate
a forest,
but fail.
You can see them
failing
at different heights
above.

Now, a waterfall of light
drenches us.

Outside a hut
with a bright blue
thatched roof.

Two floodlights
at the top
of long poles
light up
most
of an empty parking lot,
but an area
between the lights
remains dark.

Steam
rises
off the lake
in the sunlight.
A rowboat
is half-hidden
in the
reeds
across the lake.
It's the only boat out.

Several kinds of lettuce
are lit by a psychedelic light.
Everything white
turns purple.
And everything green
turns black.
And is
immediately forgotten.
But the purple
cannot be forgotten.
It is the light

of our
illusionary,
illusionist,
elusory,
elusive
world.

The true light,
the blinding light,
comes from
over there.

A tall polite man,
the next visitor.

July 16, 2007 (later)

▼

A boy walks
around a circular pool.

A group chases
but can't catch
a cloud of green gas.

An island
reflects light
like a mirror.
The island
is a mirror,
embedded
in another mirror.
Is that mirror
embedded
in another mirror?

French fries
point every which way
on a
blue plastic plate.
Salt grains
glow
in a salt shaker,
glow and enlarge.

I cross a humped
bridge
at night.
A few fish
swim
in the absolute darkness

under the bridge.
They're not
herbivores.

A matronly woman
is lit
by the inside light
of a refrigerator.
The sink's faucet
is unusually long.
A man
in a white T-shirt
sits
at the end of a bench.

A white doll
glows
in a small box
on the floor
in a dark room.
A kitten's head
glows
on the floor
in the dark room.
There's nothing afterward.
A hotdog stand
on a corner
with a big umbrella,
an umbrella
you can lose yourself under.

Her mouth expresses such
skepticism,
such uncertainty.
It seems to go up and down like a seesaw.
And the sky

has turned a shade too blue,
a never-seen blue.
They walk
behind brown bushes.
Dead bushes.

A white light
flashes,
the flasher
at the end
of a jetty.
Lights flashing in the harbor,
that was important to us
for some reason.
That was something
we could talk about endlessly.

The sun shines
through a black wrought-iron gate.
This is not a healthy place.
A cloud
crosses over the sun.
The cloud
oozes through the gate.

The proverbial fat lady
peeks
through a crack
in the floor-to-ceiling curtains
across the glass wall
of her motel room.

July 17, 2007

▼

The sun shines
on one patch of water.
You can see the sun
way down in the depths.

Something emerges
in the black night
in front of me.
Not a
person
or an animal.
Something amorphous,
a mist,
much larger than I am.

There are many shades of black,
just as there are many shades of white.
Or is it
there are many shades of white,
but only one shade of black?

A brown horse
is saddled and waiting.
My eye
falls
on some straw
in the corner of the stall.

Why does this
particular galaxy
seem
so bright?

A green light,
a small yellow-green light,
flashes
across the lake.
One time and never again.
You might think I made it up.

In the passageway
outside the sleeping compartments,
the train window
is open a little at the top.
A man
flicks cigarette ashes
out the opening.

My elbow
emits a strange glow,
as if giving birth to stars.

We haven't gotten anywhere,
except perhaps
to a place where
the stars are
so thickly
sown
they might light
the way for us
on the plain below.
But we can't descend
to the plain below.
That isn't necessarily a bad thing.

These small clouds,
crab-shaped,
dust-colored,

float down toward the ground,
brighten as they near the ground.

July 18, 2007

▼

There's a tall
light tower.
It casts
a very faint light.

Lips—
the only feature
visible.
I can't tell
whether it's
a man's face
or a woman's face.

An image
in the depths
I can't reach.

The Torah.

A strong sun
shines down
through
a leafy tree.
I walk past doorways
in an ancient city
carved out of rock.
With red roses
and silver roses
where the sun
breaks through.
With high walls
that our minds
can't

scale.
We only know
it is very bright
within.

And sometimes,
it pays
not to get the most of me,
I hear a man say.
That's an inner voice.

A runner passes,
an orange blur.

July 19, 2007

▼

They have monkeys
dancing
in the brown water.

Lime
spikes
of light
define
a virtual walkway.

She throws back
her red hair,
her breasts.

They watch now
from the upper tiers
in the big tent.
The sky hound,
a man's voice says.

July 23, 2007

▼

A man looks into a box
of green and silver Christmas balls.
Silver coins
glint in the light.

Heads look down
from a circular gallery.
Bald or shaved heads, all of them.

Still a few raspberries
hide among the leaves.
There are faces
in the smoke
billowing up
into the starry night.
Faint silhouettes
of large trees.
Why do a few bright greens
flash out of the darkness?

A bird with a long neck.
An animal with a mustache
and beard.
A monkey or dog.
These frosty blues and purples
aren't an accident.
They are a man in armor,
a horse in armor.
They're fighting a giant bird,
which is exactly the same colors.
It is the dawn of a day,
or the utter dusk.

Small meteors
rain on us
in the endless night.

I remember her.
She
has an orange balcony,
with vines growing up to it.
She has an elephant blanket.

The light tower flares—
and then goes dark.
There is a player on this team who is not over 18.

Afternoon sunlight
filters down
through
thick sugar maples,
a fine rain
by the time it reaches
the forest floor.
There's a dog
or a fox
or a possum
hiding
right over there.

A fish
enters a man's face.
Two men's faces,
close,
yelling at each other,
butting each other,
like
Egon Schiele and Gustav Klimt
in Schiele's painting.

A blue flash
above the oily shallows'
rainbow colors—
a sky-blue butterfly.

Now a whole kids group
exercises together,
the leader
with a whistle around his neck.
And that is a donkey.
And that is a demon.
And that is a bear.
And that is a cloud,
shaped like an avenging angel.
And that is a bear.
And that is a monkey.
And that
is some wizened
small animal.
And that
is a salamander's face,
almost a blank slate.
And that is a street corner,
the store
closed for the night.
Why is that person looking into the store?

All those kids,
sitting by the lockers,
changing
after gym.

There's this unstoppable sun here.
It shines into everything.
The tip of a tree caught fire.

Snow was on all the trees,
all the green leaves.
Those fiends started telling me yesterday.

Colored dots
flourish in the night—
purple
and green
and yellow.

Everything droops,
hangs down
in these dark hallways.
A tiny skull
floats toward me.
Then a South American man
with a
tangerine bandanna.

July 23, 2007 (later)

▼

A tugboat
leads a black ocean liner
to a pier
at night.

People's energy
emanates
from below the knees.

The ladder
up the side
of the brick building
is too steep.
The ladder
is made of light.
Imagine a world
in which everything
is made of light.

The light
snows down
from an unexpected
window.
Globs of mercury
line the
edges
of this window.
The edges of this pond.

July 30, 2007

II

▼

A bright green lawn slopes down under tall trees

A big black car parks right up against a store
Near skinny trees with yellow leaves
People sit there on a log bench, waiting
You just need to show them the shortcut

A horse with a bright yellow head and no features

A flower shrinks into a cube of sugar

She has bright yellow eyelashes
Her image wavers on a yellow pool
It doesn't exist, or nothing exists

We're looking at the backs of buildings that front on Commonwealth
    Ave.

A watch falls to the bottom of a lake

An insect with two bright yellow antennae and black dots on top
Streaky yellow clouds overhead

A building has a glass tower on one side
The tower's roof looks like a pointed German helmet
Long curtains hang down, motionless, stirred by no breeze
People went out back to a pool
A circular pool
A yellow pool
A pool of light

The readers aren't there, the writers aren't there
The inkholders at the desks are empty
The university must be on break
The English university
A road sign across the street reads: REDUCE SPEED AHEAD
A minivan is parked near the sign

A path under low trees along a chain-link fence
Like the path back to the parking lot from the ocean side of Montauk
    Point

The camera freezes on a large tree trunk, a silver maple
A gold dot breaks free from the vegetation and floats overhead
The gold dot watches us
The vegetation has almost swallowed the brown church
Trees must be growing in its nave

She wears a black shawl on top of her high forehead

The inside of his mouth...was...light silver
They're wrapping bandages around his head
Dirty bandages
From one of our past wars

This smelly white being near the ceiling
A flying monkey
Pure white, pure white fur
Such delicate white hands, white fingers

A young woman with short blonde hair, holding a coffee cup, climbs
    on a bus

We have people sailing in different places along the shadowy bank of
    a river

The yellow tide spreads over the ground

His nose is made of deep purple triangles
Deep purple stained-glass triangles

And now what is it time for?

A smooth black wall
With cloudy yellows embedded in it
The metal doors of a mausoleum
Deep shade
Permanent moisture
Hemlock needles

A teapot with the head of a laughing old man

July 28, 2008

▼

There's a man with a goatee
A few gray hairs among the stringy black hairs

A bicycle racer, bearing down on me, seems to have wings
All of them bearing down on me seem to have wings
Manmade wings, not angel wings or bird wings

Water bubbles on the right side of a pond

Sketchy beings
Sketchy mountains
Sketchy seaways
It's darker than usual
Electricity lights the sky and the sea at night
A man has dressed up as a giant flower
His face just a small point in the middle of a gigantic rose
How can his neck support so much weight?

A gray horse's head against a blue night sky
The head evaporates
A cloud is lit by the moon it obscures

A flame shoots out the top of a volcano, out of someone's head, out
    of a cigarette lighter
The flame turns into a broad ray of light shining down

Two black phone lines cross below overhanging vines
An old car pulls into the place
A horseman rides into the place
A big black spider appears at night
He knew there was a big black spider in the darkness
When is it so dark we can't see a thing?

A multicolored elk
A multicolored sheep
A glowing white mushroom enlarges and then shrinks
A bush in the middle of the forest has a milky glow
Ghostly
They are beings trying to get back
Coming to an event
At the top of the sky
I can't make out what or who they are
They're puffs, tufts, like transitory clouds

A house comes into view, only for a moment
Clouds sail rapidly overhead in the darkness
It's all clouds now
But somewhere off to the left, a world is beginning

A horse, all caparisoned, heads toward me in a blond light
The carriage heads toward me, at a processional speed

This huge egg of light weighs the hemlock branches down to the
      ground
This huge egg of light, not the egg of a dinosaur, but the egg of a hill,
      weighs down this corner of the house
The fish's open mouth is fluorescent
The pig's head, the horse's head, glow
The racers have green wings and a transparent bubble for a head
I could duck under their wings and avoid being run over
The small carved crèche glows
The hippopotomus's lower jaw glows
The cow, cat and owl glow

Silver liquid runs down the rocks
Near a narrow yellow house
Hills in the distance beyond the steep roof
I don't know where I am
And I don't know where I'm going

August 4, 2008

▼

The tentacles of a jellyfish hang down over me in the black water

A Joseph Albers painting: a small yellow square, surrounded by a larger
    black square, surrounded by a larger charcoal square

There are feet walking, many feet walking, on muddy ground
A door swings open and closed, open and closed
An eye looks back at me, a very dark eye, through a mist

A dark horse rides off into the dark sky
With a...slumped rider
Both are soaked

A clownish woman stifles a smile, which makes me smile even more
People help each other clean up a mess
A gold hat, a witch's hat, floats upward
A streamer, tiny and black, along the horizon
Storms of light
We're leaving through that door

A black mushroom, a white mushroom
Another white mushroom
A white T-shirt hanging in a closet
A white leaf
Two white sails in the distance

An upside-down woman's head, a Madonna
A little red man slides down the birth canal
He shakes his head at us
A shock of blond hair
It's ridiculous

A thumb jabs at something
Bright yellow liquid drains into the hole in the black

August 12, 2008

▼

A sketch of a person confronts me

I saw this woman in a painting by Vuillard
She wore a long dress
Everything about her was long
Every inch of her skin was covered

You can't see the trees for the forest
The spruces, especially two of them, touch the sky and keep going
You could climb them into another world, a world all white

A cranberry sky above the mountains
An orange sun drips down the cranberry sky toward a notch

She sits up straight, with her back to the wall, in a very yellow room
Her shawl is bright red, electric
Her necklace bright red
An orange face wants to emerge from the fluorescent night

Above us is the hole where the extinct volcano opens to the sky
The sky comes all the way down to us at the bottom of the cone

Of course, she is wearing a brown fur hat, a cylindrical hat

August 14, 2008

▼

The world is a red tie with black and yellow paisley designs
A green light on a boat in the harbor at night
A blue light, the most beautiful deep-blue light, not far away

A pile of sneakers by the door
A shirtless man and his son walking outside
Each with a towel draped over one of his forearms
Soon, the man will wear it around his waist

A turtle, made of light, rears up and leans against a white wall

They're not going to go. We're not going to come.

An older man, a sweet version of Robert Frost
My wife Louisa's Uncle Nate Shiverick, "Mr. Cigarette"
A beagle sleeps on the floor near a fireplace
It makes me feel warm just looking at it
And tall glasses on glass tables, beaded with water
And a couple of coffee table books
One with aerial views of the Earth
That would be the best coffee table book to have
And photos taken through microscopes

In the red night, under a curved roof
A passageway that doesn't lead anywhere
Or anywhere important, in any way, to anyone

A man carries apples, bright red apples in both hands
They glint almost as much as his body armor glints

They sit on monstrous tall-backed chairs
Above all of us
Faces on silver coins
Sinking in the black water

August 15, 2008

▼

A yellow top hat floats on a dark pool at night
It's not time yet
Sue Straussberg, a girl I knew in childhood, looks at me
The clouds will be lit, if nothing else
The clouds will be gold-tinted
Light leaks out of the ground, out of cracks in the ground, holes in the
    ground

A rider, on a dark brown horse, sits and waits
A drop of moisture on the reins glints in the sun

Someone reaches out, over a precipice, to pick a wildflower

There, underwater, the duck
His two arms...stir up...so much muck
This hooked fish won't let itself be reeled in

He turns into a white flag, flapping in the wind
The white flag has two black eyes, each looking off to the side
L'oblivione ingombra i miei pensieri

A dog looks at me, with a large gold head, and a white nose
A whiteness we're not supposed to see, not supposed to know about
There's another animal in the mix
A silver dog with a very straight back
It points straight up at the sky
Its fluffy silver tail hangs all the way down to the ground
There's sun up there
Sky up there
Far up above the tops of the trees
We can't worry about it
We can only be comforted by the fact that it's there

We have no concept of how much white fur is needed to make this
  cape
A white fish sticks its head out of the water
A white seahorse
A white carousel horse with a white post through its body

An opera covers the night sky
A mythology, gods and goddesses
It doesn't make much sense

A window is swallowed by the night

The surface of the world looks like the surface of the brain
Gray with curving lines scored in it

A cream-colored balloon will carry us into the sky

A face, Richard Nixon's, almost emerges on the dark screen

A man with a derby hat sits at the steering wheel
I can't make out his features at night
He's looking at something
A gold bracelet with a clasp in the shape of a snakehead
It has jeweled eyes, ruby eyes

A little monkey with a very white face and white hair looks around
He wants to know what happened here
He tips back his head, so he can look straight up at the sky
The little fellow, I shouldn't worry about him

August 16, 2008

▼

The sky is blue-black behind his left arm
Cocked to throw a javelin

Three men are bent over a small fire on the rocks, blowing on it

My childhood friend Steve Kurens' father, head bent over, looks at
    something on a low table
So much dark wood here, Roaring Twenties splendor
My childhood next-door neighbor, Lynn Brodie, and her cat
The brook by the abandoned Board of Education building

A pink dog's head, a pink horse's head, a pink possum's head
A pink bear came into our tarp in the middle of the night
A pink bear with big black circles around its eyes, raccoon eyes

A string of lights hangs down from a blinding roof

Cornstalks look like they're about to whack us on the head
They look mean today

A raspberry sky above the rooftops
The tops of the trees are fuzzy
We might not be able to stay here, though I don't understand why

Somewhere within these caves, in a vaulted room
Like the inside of a sombrero
We have not come here

A big animal is tethered to the ground through its nose, an ox
Something brutal and degraded about it

Lapis lazuli there
Lapis lazuli
Lapis
As I say that, a blue crystal tower rises toward the sky
A pinnacle

After a while, I come up with her smile in the darkness
A black ghost flies over the water
A flying gorilla
A gigantic crow
It skims the mountaintops, leaves a little blue visible between it and
    the ridge

I don't have to look for much
It's all there
Is there anything more to see now?
Two women, with white-blonde bird heads
A tiny silver dot that leads into some other dimension
Without knowing better, I want something to come down for me

A yellow cat, very fluffy, leans against a yellow wall on a blue night
A tenuous rope bridge crosses the blue night, constantly breaking and
    re-forming

August 17, 2008

▼

There's a secret green place in the night
A blue ring hangs on a peg on a wall
A few yellow trees, each leaf a light

A tall lit cross on the roof of a barn
The light lives at the bottom of a deep well
In the perpetual shade for centuries

We're not sure where we are now
Sometimes that's a good thing

Listen to the water: it's close to high tide

In this light, I can't find what I seek

Every door is outlined by light
Every window is outlined by light
I'm not sure what I should look at
One window is as small and thin as a pencil
The light outside the window is silver
Now I look through a triangular keyhole
I see bright white, a boy with curly hair

August 22, 2008

▼

She nods her head, it's a simple as that

The back of a red Ford Mustang pokes out of a garage
A garage with a small copper onion dome

An empty tall-back chair on the right side of a featureless room
A wooden salad spoon
The part in his white-blonde hair
The orange wall against which our wildest dancing is projected

A yellow emergency vehicle swerves left into a canyon road

A blond boy throws rocks into the water
"Don't throw rocks," I say to the boy, "You'll hurt the—"
I'm not sure what I'm afraid he'll hurt

An orange cloud above us tonight
A dark room with an orange ceiling and static in the air
A rope ladder unrolls down the black wall from the orange ceiling
The table begins to glitter, its top and sides and legs

August 25, 2008

▼

The sun is shining in my eyes
In the window of the next cabin, a man smiles
I can't tell who he is, in the sun
I see the back of a boy as he walks toward the sun
Is it possible to walk up the trunk of a tree into the sun?
Instead of sinking below the horizon, the sun seems to bounce up and
      down on the horizon

The train has a horizontal silver stripe
The train is a horizontal silver stripe

The island is sinking

He stands against the wall near an arched doorway, in the weak light
A gold belt buckle catches the light
The light leaves a scar on the back of a car
The plum-covered trunk above the bumper
A headdress slides down one side of his head
The filigree

But we still point toward the sun
A gold stain
A gold spider
A gold maple leaf

Wisteria has grown between them and the world
Between their balconies and the world

The sun rises on a peacock's tail
The sun rises on each peacock feather
The sun rises far away

The sun set a long time ago
An ice cream sandwich lies on a table at night
There's no better beginning

A chicken struggles just out of view
A sense of light, heat, a few feathers in the air

We waited in the heat outside the train station in Tarquinia for the bus
    up to the town and the Etruscan tombs

That's a live wire on the right

A brightly lit restaurant floats in the middle of the night
Reflected on water

September 1, 2008

▼

Night has a nose
A long nose
With big nostrils
And a moustache?
I don't think we can verify that
Just as I'm hesitant to talk about the teeth
This is a good vision
I think I'll keep it

I think I see
Salmonella
On a piece of ham
It's the shape of a typical lake

A cross-country skier
Emerges from a trail
Through
Spruce trees

A few hooks
Hang down
From the edge
Of a roof
What are they for?

Night breaks in waves
On the dusky scene

Night billows
Like smoke

Night reaches out its lobsterclaw
O lobster
In perpetual night
We should all swim with facemasks
Or at least kids' goggles

Two thin swords
Cross
Forming
A glowing gate
As they did
At Louisa's grandparents' wedding
In 1924

September 3, 2008

▼

I see a city in the distance at night
A city downriver at night
A dull gold awning

So far, the black seems blacker
The sidewalk turns to the left
It's a yellow day
A sandy colored day
A garbage can is turned upside-down
And things
Keep
Falling out of it
Some lighter than air
They never reach the ground
....this green world at night
I'm just not gonna worry what it's like, where it's going

She stands far down the train platform
Way at the end of the train platform
Where only the longest trains ever stop
It is not one of those proverbial January nights
Waiting on the platform at Princeton Junction
With a cigarette bummed from Lisa Sabbatini

Between this and that
Sulfurous yellow mold on a wall
....
Bring this back
....
I'm walking into darkness
Slightly able to see where I'm going
The images are few and far between
Half-lit

Jagged walls
Of a canyon
The Milky Way
At the end of the tunnel
Men and women separated by a black mass outlined in light

....

It has a gold aura

A plant peeks out of the Earth

September 4, 2008

▼

It's very black outside
There's a tunnel
A house above the tunnel
A swimming pool to its right
Lit up
I hate these places

Now I see inside a steel mill
Molten metal

A red tricycle on the sidewalk
New concrete
The kind that stands out
Whiter than everything around it

The large woman sitting at a round table makes a face
Who can ever understand it?
Is there more to see?
A cloudy sky
A bicycle parked against a brick wall
A feeling of wobbliness as I look up at the sky
Haloes around heads
A tan woman
In a slinky yellow dress
Sitting at a table
With others
Turns her palm up
As if to say,
"What?"

I'm not involved in that
I'm not going to be part of that
I'm not going to be there

I see
I can understand that
Some of us aren't going to be there

September 5, 2008

▼

We're sitting inside a car
At night
Lit by the light
Streaming from stores
On both sides of the street
A dead main street
In suburbia
On a weeknight

I'm standing on the side of a basketball court
Half-watching
People play
Half-waiting

The sun disappears behind tall factory buildings
There's plenty of time left in the afternoon
A whole evening and night ahead

Red taillights back out of an alley

September 6, 2008

▼

I have no idea what I'm seeing
Except that it's very bright
Like headlights
Motorcycle headlights
A swarm of motorcycle headlights
Black motorcycles
Black and white

The Lord does not have mercy on us today
The Lord is not our shepherd today

A boy laughs raucously, almost maniacally
Like an animal
A primate
We are in deadly danger in this environment

The madness of David Foster Wallace

The mailman drives up
To the little mailbox
On the country road
His teeth are pearls
Each tooth is a pearl

When she bends over I see a brown baby on her back
A second baby grows out of her left shoulder
A cat grows out of her nose

Trees reach down into the ocean and pick up the fishing nets

All those gold heads
Marching into the sun
Gold-painted hair

Gold-painted skin
Gold-painted clothes

More bees than people

*You can see these poor construction guys can't finish tearing up the street
        as fast as they'd like*

The weak sunlight
Falls on the
Frieze
Drawing our attention
To the horses
The horses were most important
The horses were the stars
Each of those horses was famous
Its exploits known
Like a baseball player's or football player's

In a train station
A lady looks like my former colleague Barb Haislip
But wearing a straw hat
With a huge brim
This might be a vision
Of a moment far in the past
Even before my lifetime

He stood up to those demonstrators
*The governor stood up to the demonstrators in the office and coming out
        of the stairway*

The afternoon is olive green
The drab green
Of a military camp
A muddy military camp
In a long-past war

A great chewing seems to be taking place
A yellow and purple chewing
...of mowed grass
Bristly

Who's that kid smiling?
That kid with a crewcut?
Jogging out of my field of vision
Jogging out of the cabin
A collision
A mother and son
Hugging in the mustardy light

Rodin's Victor Hugo
Maybe a burgher of Calais in the background

What light is this at night?
Everything minutely lit up, though the overall effect is one of darkness

The kids at the back of the group
On the dimming Little League field
Hold up
Blue candles
Not lit
A train rattles by toward New York
It is going to be tomorrow soon

Multicolored feathers grow out of the ground
Like small leaves
In the white sunlight

The light shines here and there
On each rider as they pass
On the rider's right hand
On the rider's right stirrup
On the horse's back flank

A 19th century forest of ship masts
At night
Lightning in the distance
Seeming to pick out
One mast
Or another
In an optical illusion

A gnomish man
Tilts his head upward in the night

An elephant
With widely spaced teeth

In this
Cosmically lit
Night
The stars
Fall
Like snow
I know
I will look outside
In the morning
And the world
Will be covered
With several inches
Of stars
The surface of the world
Will be covered with stardust

As long as our nights
Snow stars
America cannot die
Ain't that right?

Is there something beyond the end here?
Black trying to emerge
But a silver cloud
A film of silver
Won't allow it

September 15, 2008

▼

The world is dark green
With a face trying to emerge
The face of Lenin, or someone of his generation
Very pale, pale white
Forehead and cheeks

A profusion of asparagus fern
In the window

I feel like I'm looking at the world through a bottle of limeade
I see a train station across a plain
Somewhere in Italy or Mexico
At a dead time of day

I sense insects
In the darkness
The edges of things
Have been electrified
And light up

September 16, 2008

▼

One light illuminates a county airport runway at night
A car passes an empty parking lot, heading for Dunkin' Donuts

Through large windows, a calm ocean and pale blue sky

The faintest spotlight on the blackest stage
The faintest spotlight on the blackest curtain slowly fades out

The green night out the picture window quickly turns black

We have soul stirrings today
An old Chinese man sits at a rough table in a hut

The moon shines on the river below the tip of the long island
He senses a boat passing, but there's no boat in sight

An A-frame in the shady woods at camp in Maine 40 years ago
A tall trellis on the left of the front door
Flowers bloom in my face
I can't see my way around them
They are all around me, a friendlier thought than it sounds

Inside a geodesic dome, lit by an orange light
A vague force tosses a vaguer rider
Little more than a puff of dark smoke

A small window in the middle of a dark wall
Outside, indeterminate night

July 9, 2009

▼

A rider seems to be falling off
A horse on a starry night
But he never does fall off

Two dogs fight in the darkness
Two dogs made of light

A sledge speeds away at night

A flower has a small eye of light

Pots bubble on every burner
In the dim kitchen
Of the dim apartment

Birches droop under a dim circus tent
Girls dance onstage many decades ago

Sitting in the darkness, watching
We could drift off to sleep
The air weighs on us
The green sky overhead

July 13, 2009

▼

A drummer stands under a white spotlight, the only person onstage
A bright p is written on the black curtain

Looking down from the top of a tall building, I see an oil tanker in a
    river
Looking down from a very tall building, I see a dancer eddying, then
    slowly floating downstream, like Ophelia
Truly, I am seeing phantoms, inner phantoms

I see the dark arches of a viaduct in Riverside Park
Something truly beautiful, a foggy pink moon on the waters
And then, after it's blotted out, just the waters

Now the lights of Time Square beckon

In this X-ray of the neck, there are far too many green spaces
In this X-ray of the body cavity, there's a dark cloud

Things are broken on the floor
The porch chair at night
Late at night

At what point do we just float downstream?

Look, I see my second cousin Lisi Schoenbach

July 17, 2009

▼

There are trillions of dim stars
None brighter than the others

Small currents in the darkness
More felt than seen

A store in France around World War I
Why do I think of the past as dusty?
Bouquets of flowers outside the store
Statues in the middle of a fountain
Chalky white, pocked by acid rain

A man in a derby hat stands in front of me
Waiting to hand me something

Two rivers flow together at night
It's a memory of Bayonne
The night is framed at the bottom by a forearm

A plane sits in the dim light
Of a county airport closed for the night

July 21, 2009

▼

The sky is sprinkled with lime stars
Grains of salt float down

Headlights paint us sloppily
Lit clouds come toward us from down the road

We're walking toward Grindstone Point in Maine
A car emerges from West Oval on the right
Speeds toward us, screeches to a stop
We all run

We never knew who it was

Two trucks press against each other, in front of a white sky
Like they're going to fight, hood to hood, hoodpiece to hoodpiece
But we have to move on
A glacier spills out of the mountains
A glacier spills from the sky
Empties the sky

I'm in a marsh out West
Along the Snake River in Wyoming
Where it's both dry and wet

There's this great unity
I don't know what it is
The sun shining over mountains
Shining in my eyes

The police car with the realistic dummy
Parked near the general store in Teasdale, Utah
One late afternoon in July 2006

An intensely blonde woman speaking
Almost white blonde
A 1940s hairstyle
With blinding white fields beyond her

A man with a moustache
Leans against a screen-porch post
He looks like my long-dead brother David
He smiles...sheepishly? Shyly?

A man's forehead
The rest of the face doesn't take form
But the forehead
And the hair thrown back
Remind me of Louisa's cousin Tommy Bruce

People throng the battlements
Of a squat tower

July 27, 2009

▼

A starry sky approaches at the speed of light
With a hole in the middle

Bright sunlight on a shed roof
Painted by Van Gogh in Arles

A dark ladder at night
Doesn't lean
Against anything
Except the moon

The sky can't be faulted for splitting
Sometimes the sun erupts from below

I wouldn't be surprised to see
Swans
Floating
Among these
Deep green reflections
But there aren't any

Toppled trees
Lie straight down
The steep riverbank
White birches
I saw them at camp in Maine

I'm looking through underbrush
For someone or something

A long curving field in spring
Seedlings planted in brown mud
Overcast, threatening

A giant bird
Stands on a ledge
Outside a window at night
The bird even darker
Than the night sky

August 3, 2009

▼

Someone is splashing in the water
A few feet away from a dock
Drowning, I fear

A hand of sunlight
Has made it through
All the trees
And touched the water
Is there an image at the bottom of the water?

A middle-aged man from the 1960s
In black and white
Like Lyndon Johnson
But not Lyndon Johnson

The darkness frightens me
With its dim square of light in the middle
A very dim room in Kafka's "The Trial"

An older blonde woman watches a sailing race through binoculars

A small fountain sends up three powerful jets
Secluded like the fountains
In the woods behind Versailles

August 12, 2009

▼

A door is reflected in water at night

A trickle of a waterfall
Begins high above us

A sideview mirror glints in the sun

A boy wears a purple triangular hat

The day turned bright yellow
It crept up to them
It swept over them
Over the low houses
And garages
The low telephone poles

A monumental sculpture
Rains light on the people below
Light rains against the tall windows
Behind the balconies of European cities

Each flagstone on the walk
Has been painted white

A small plane waits on a runway

Two women cook in the kitchen
With bare upper arms
Something preemptory about their movements
So in control

A dark pink tank on the wall
Holds cold liquid
Or cold gas

August 21, 2009

▼

We see the world through pale blue smoke
There's no good answer

A person is slipping off a cliff
Losing his handhold
It's a slapstick movie

He's trying to fix something in the small room
The small room filled with tools
What is inside the black box?

The letter L made of thick black lines

A window on a lavender world
A lavender sky

The Earth
Far below
Is a very unusual color of green
Spinach green
Dark blue green

The fence slats look white in the sun

What does this little dog want?

A blonde woman is smiling
Two little kids stand beside her right knee

A black church rises in a green wood

A dark vehicle in the darkness

Half of the sky has end-of-sunset colors
The other half is pitch black

No confusion greater, no longing greater

The man bends over a paint can
Stirs it with a stick

Through a notch, a valley, a distant valley

A seated older woman motions with her arms
As if to say, "Enough! That's enough!"

Gray smoke billows through a hole
Into a black room

August 22, 2009

▼

A lion in a cage
A cartoon lion
It's night
The scene is bathed
By a strange green light
Both dim and energetic

A gigantic wing of feathery clouds covers one-fourth of the sky

A large water bird takes off from the surface of a swamp, making a
    commotion
It rises above the dead trees

Two blinding points of light reflect off the shield of a medieval soldier

This window is bright
The string from the shade hangs down and divides the room into two
    parts
A room in an apartment
Vuillard might have painted

The sun, concealed by darkness, is nonetheless there

A ladder leans against a tree at night
Bathed in silver-white light

The power lines are down
Wires cross each other
On this rainy fall morning
A green and yellow morning

Look at the fish in the fish tanks in the store window

It's hard to see anymore

An old man's face, carved on a half moon

A large dog is trying to get into the room
But not threatening
Part of a tableau
An Iwo Jima-like tableau

September 18, 2009

▼

Monorail tracks curve in the sky overhead
Crossing at different heights

A flimsy ladder of light
Hangs down
From a hole
In the night sky

Through scrubby trees
A tennis court

A train runs along the flat ridge of a mountain range to the east
Soon the sun will rise

Purple wild grapes
Lend their color
To the
Sluggish stream
Down below

Tiny volcanoes
Grow out of a dark wall at night

Yellow lines delineate the petals and complex center
Of the black rose

September 21, 2009

▼

A trembling white pyramid
Rises out of the black ocean
The black night

A pyramid made of salt
A flimsy pyramid
You can almost see through it

The wake is a cloud of stars

This stoplight has only one color, white
It shines in your eyes, masters you
The stream of light
Coming toward you
Breaks into two streams
Two thin streams
That flow off
To the left
And the right

An identical ship is docked
At every pier
They look unreal
From out in the river
An optical illusion

We look at a Middle Eastern country from far above

Two electric sockets at the bottom of a wall

Piano keys
Reflected on trembling water at night
Dim lines of light

A narrow glowing canoe on a beach
A face behind it all
With a floppy moustache
Like the Yankees' Thurman Munson
Who died in a small plane crash
Or a big dog

An olive green door
Empty towel racks

The back window of a car

September 24, 2009

▼

A bird
A big parrot
Sits next to a man
In a bright blue seat
At a stadium

I'm on a riverboat
With vast crystal chandeliers
How many pieces are in that chandelier?

So there was this wagon train traveling at night
In the artificial moonlight
Never has moonlight looked so artificial

The light left a scar
In the darkness
The light scarred the night

A white turban glows in the dark
I can't see the head
Much less the body
Of the person wearing it
Only the turban
Floating in the dark
An igloo

There were fireworks
Above a carnival at night
The sky caught fire
What should you do when the sky catches fire?

We've been invited to look down on the sea
This small whirlpool

September 25, 2009

▼

I have entered a land of gold auras
Nights of gold static

A horse in the distance
In the sunny field beyond the fence

A troop rides toward me on horses
With their bells and whistles
A multitude
Riding into a city
Like in a Renaissance print

There's a light half of the room
And a dark half of the room
The light half on the right
A mixture of lime green and gray

Was that lightning?

Animals fight in the dark
They make me twitch

Frogs with glowing faces in the water at night
Wolves with glowing faces
Their teeth bared
In the water at night

Something at the end of the darkness
A small gold statue shining
A statue of a star

A gigantic black mushroom grows in the night
Inexplicable light
Lights up one area or another of the ocean

Where does the light come from
that faintly lights the ceiling
and no other part of the room?

A loud river at the bottom of the ravine

A white stripe
Straight down the middle of the night
A crude white stripe
That dissolves back into the night

A car drives away
In a wooded suburb
A bit of exhaust in the air

A strip of photos

Slot machines spinning

A red door with a blue doorknob
And then slowly, the room turns bright yellow

A tan high rise is reflected in a lake
A glowing tan high rise
An old car drives along the edge of the lake
A '50s Buick

For once, I can see everything
The tiny reticulations

Whatever it is
Armor
Rocks
Tufts of grass
Wildflowers
A cliff

A great confusion
At the bottom of a cloud castle

Light reaches into this nether world
Through a ground-floor window
A silver light

A fake highway
With fake signs
Brighter than normal colors
Everything made of plastic
More signs than needed

I'm floating in a dreamland here
With dark terrapin clouds
A school of turtles

Outside in a garden at night
Big-leaved tropical plants overhead

A snowy field rising at night
Green in the moonlight

A small purple square
In the middle of the dark green
It slowly disappears

There are things I don't know
Can never understand

What is over the waterfall
In the foggy canyon?

Up the driveway
Inside the porch on the right side of house

The sleeper is restless
Bombarded in a way
We are not bombarded
In waking life
Little surprise
The sleeper writhes

Before steep cliffs
In a Utah national park

A horizontal white board in the middle of the black
It expands
It contracts
It rotates
It begins to turn into a flower

A bright purple box
The most beautiful color in the world
In the middle of a pale-lime circle
And then black beyond
Purple box, lime circle, black beyond

Now a three-dimensional baroque effect
Vines hung over stone fences

Moonlight on a swampy lake

A silver animal
With antlers
So festooned
With flowers and vines
I can't tell
Which animal it is

Something very complex
Carved from ivory
A gargoyle
Emerging from the crotch
Of a larger figure
Leaning back in a chair
Boccioni's "La Risata"

Lying on my back
At the bottom of a pool
I can see everything happening above me

The sun splinters into a world of gold fountains
Giant gold snowflakes break off the upper branches of the fountains
Fall and catch on the lower branches

There's something about the way the light illuminates
The partly open theater curtain
The Victorian house with a turret visible onstage
It seems to light up more than three dimensions
It's like you can see four dimensions of the scene
Would that be time-lapse photography?
A movie?

The trail comes out into the open
High orchards
Stone fence posts

People stream
Into the tall arched doorway
Of a castle

An animal
Poses on top of a ladder
In a fancy room
Like in a Velasquez painting

Is it a dog?
It has big ears that point straight up
It's a rabbit
With the face of
Mad Magazine's Alfred E. Neuman

A weathered face
Lincoln's face
Ringed by hair

Now a gorilla's face

Something hideous
A dead cow's face
A monster's face
A huge bird or dragon towering over me

I'm floating in a dreamland here
I saw some things—what were they?
Rural places, fields and hills
As far as the eye can see
What do we see or hear?
It's early dawn or late dusk
Astral dawn or astral dusk

A brilliant patch of light on the path

A lit-up wall
Rough concrete
Maybe the side of a museum

A bright area in the middle of the night sky

As the ivy grows up our fences
We become almost incapable of moving

Something is going to happen
In the center of this dust

What you want are the branches of small trees
With small fruits
The color of nectarines
But smaller

The brightness of certain places
Certain corridors
Shocks me
I don't know how to live in these spaces
That section of the street is just too bright
Why is it so bright?
Is there a phone booth there?
A bus stop?

The clouds come from different places
They have different agendas
I don't fully understand
How they fit together
Except that they do fit together
And the wind is....

Was that a shooting star?
Is this the astral light at the end of sunset?

Is it possible everything is made of feathers?
Everything has feathers sticking out
The chairs, the walls, the rugs
Is that possible?
Tawny feathers
The color of lions

Whose face struggles to come into view?
Paul von Hindenburg's

Can anything but slugs flourish in this moist land?

Mold or signs of wetness
On the walls in the dark

Just a cloud above a chariot
Both...who knows when
...across the ceiling
All the...
All the grand dining rooms

Are we each riding elephants?
A soldier's face
A woman's face
With very pointed features
In the...

Is there a white face in the midst of the darkness?
Long white beard
Long white locks
One eye
In the middle of the head
Surrounded by a triangle

September 28, 2009

IV

▼

A bright yellow bird
outlined in bright red
flies across the top
of the black sky

A monkey stands
on a bare branch

There is a giant arch
above the landscape
a plastic rainbow

A face wants to emerge
a moose-faced boy
a moose-faced girl

July 8, 2010

▼

The most beautiful blue, yellow and red
a large blue fish
and a smaller yellow fish
which turns into a red fish

The blue fish disappears
and there's only the red fish

July 8, 2010 (later)

▼

A gold bar
glows on the ground
in a dark room

We watch
the roof
of a convertible
retracting

A snowshoe
mounted on a wall
in a dark room

This man has a screen for a face
with words written on it

I think there's something
at the bottom
of the swirling water
But there never is

July 12, 2010

▼

We're floating in a canoe
in the shade
under lakeside trees

A black letter E
against a black background
black on black

A long dusty cloud
hangs above the horizon
of the ocean at dusk

You will no more see anything
through those slats
than you will—

A black woman singer
with very short hair
nods to the audience

Bars border the window
but they don't block
the window itself

They're over there
outside
in the dark
two seated
one standing

July 13, 2010

▼

A man sits
in a corner
of a dark room

He has a green aura
around his head
and body

Even the bottom rung
of the ladder
is too high
for anyone
to reach

July 14, 2010

▼

Something hides
in the darkness
beyond the darkness

The figure of a gold dancer
Emerges out of stardust

A window looks out
on a violet sky
the beginning of something
or the end of something

Searchlights rake
a raised runway

We did not follow you
to this place
the meeting
of a black mass
and a charcoal-gray mass

A child rides a bike
with training wheels
on the sidewalk
of a lush suburb

July 26, 2010

▼

I'm standing in three feet of water
Inside a dark house
The water is halfway up a window
It's very calm and peaceful
It's night outside

There's a purple dot
in the very center
of the night
in the very center
of the starry sky
overhead
I don't know
what the purple dot
could be

A ghostly light
emanates
from the outer edge
of the brain
at night

A blue light flashes
in the middle
of the left brain

The light rolls down
the left side
of the night
like a rope ladder
in a fire drill

We will not melt

in the midst

A beautiful green or blue light
makes it through the darkness

Gray light floods
through a wide doorway

I'm inside a hut
flooded like the house
but it dries up

The sunrise begins
with a giant bird
flying out of the mountains
flying out of the center
of the mountain range
Its wingspan
covers
everything visible

There's a large yellow window above me
Framed by lines of white light

August 10, 2010

▼

The night sky
is sown
with a billion stars
all flying toward me
so small
so hard to differentiate
one from the other

A motorcycle
is parked against the side
of a building
on a narrow street
in Europe
at night

Yellow steam
rises from the surface
of a lake
The surface
of the lake
spins
like a whirlpool

I think
some image
will emerge
but none does

The packed yellow center
of a flower

A large animal
made of light

walking along the road
toward us
has long sharp horns

She has large lips
pouting

Faintly illuminated
at the back
of a dark chapel
a tiny lion's face

And now she flinches
a girl who looks like Amity Shlaes
in Avignon
in late July of 1980

Chalk on a black wall
outlines
a man's body
head at the bottom
legs
going up the wall

A muffled light
in the middle
of all the darkness
A muffled moon
How quickly it fades out

An Old Master portrait of a man
One eyebrow focuses on me

August 11, 2010

▼

Many braids hang down
forming a portiere
Each braid
a braid
of darkness and light

There's a grass tennis court
and nobody playing on it
A headache
makes it hard to look
at the grass in the sun

Fran Brodie
my childhood neighbor
in a light suit
and matching light hat
and a small dog
in her arms

A searchlight runs
lovingly
up the side of a building
a concrete building
on a concrete street
with no trees
no telephone poles
no light poles

A Roman place
or a modern place
in the Southwest or Mexico

The tall grass

is going to glow
in the background
above their heads

A brightly colored quilt
hangs on a wall

August 12, 2010

▼

A blinking yellow traffic light at night
A destination at night

I look down on a basketball game
from the top of a dome
What do they call this?
A bird's-eye view?

Bright yellow smoke wafts up
from incense sticks

Look into a mirror
in the darkness

At the top of the driveway
in the garage
there's an upstairs room
half-blue
half-green
The blue seems to come
from inside the walls
and concentrates
at a fireplace

Follow the flickering light
to a maroon ladder

This shadowy being
has so many arms
with which to help people
but only two legs

A ghostly bar of light

hovers above people's heads
in the darkness

September 1, 2010

▼

The small hole at the end
of the dark tunnel
recedes in the distance

What will we call it?

A glowing cash register
People in the aisles
of a bright store

What are we going to find
in this dim light
where nothing is recognizable
and I mean nothing?
It would be better
to be in darkness
pitch darkness

Trees are reflected
in a pool of water
at dusk
wavering

Once again this dimness
a blue dimness
in which nothing is recognizable

Everything is very brown
like a Brownie's uniform

Hands reach into the mouth
of a giant stone lion
The air turns to fire

The room
was painted by Vuillard
if anyone

She shakes her head slowly
a psychologist
very reasonable

On an urban movie set at night
in the 1930s or 40s
Who am I looking at?
I'm not sure
Greer Garson?

The blonde with bright lipstick
is almost laughing
Her décolleté
right above us on the stage

September 2, 2010

▼

Donna Reed
looks up from her kitchen work
looks toward me

A man rides upside down
inside an earth-moving machine
Is the whole machine
upside down?
How and why would that be?

The sun has risen
behind those trees
behind those hills
just like sometimes
you can feel
the moon has risen
even if it hasn't
climbed above
the woods yet

Rivers of light
flow into the space

People run into a parking lot in the country
And then a huge blue pickup
drives out the back of the parking lot
into the meadow behind
It wasn't going to hit the people
It lurched away from the people
But something was threatening about it

September 20, 2010

▼

At the end of dusk
fog rises from the ground
Its upper edge seems hairy

The turbulence is a lighthouse

The moon seemed very close
in the night sky above us
a lunar module landing on us

The turbulence is the light of a train
enlarging as it nears

The turbulence is the Universal Basketball Association

July 4, 2011

▼

A window
a square of gray light
in the black
narrows into a circle
fades out altogether

Muffled yellow or pink light
seeps through the curtains
of a motel room

A very dim silhouette
of a person
seated
like Lincoln
at the Lincoln Memorial

What was that in the garish pink light?
Store windows in a strip mall

There are faint places
in the depths of the mind

An orange dot
bursts into a circular orange cloud
which lights up the ocean waters
at dawn

A maroon face
almost emerges
from the black sky
Then
a white cat
gigantic
does emerge

A brown pyramid
rises into the black sky
turns shapeless
darker
and the sky turns dark blue

A pink skeleton
floats
in the maroon water

In a black lake
with a shrinking shoreline
red jellyfish float up
out of the black depths

An orange number 6
Soon only the handle survives

A black hole
directly ahead
in the deep purple sky

It's all staging, scenery
Rarely people, situations

Thin treetops rise out of the fog
against the green-black sky
A George Innis painting

And what sights will we see now?

A bright pink turtle
flies above a black ocean
A threatening black cloud
hangs over the ocean

We are inside a black church
with a bright lavender light
inside the steeple

A black island
floats in a raspberry sea
far below us

Once again, a wooded mountainside
against a dark blue sky

We have the most lovely blue
and an orange screen or stage
far in the distance

Lovely colors
A pale blue
with a red 2x4 poking into it
but mostly the pale blue
with frosting on it
at different places
and then later
silver-edged

A field soaked with light
A dark ball in the middle

July 6, 2011

▼

A bright raspberry object
lit from several directions
hangs
in the middle
of a black space

A gray contrail
high up
in the black sky
Right beneath it
a flickering American flag
a neon American flag
with parts missing

A painting
of a bright orange sweet potato
against a dark green background
on a black wall
The sweet potato is glowing
It's in the middle of the painting
And then it fades a little bit
and turns red
and slips to the right

What are we seeing here?
A large white object
against the black
A cat
A sail
And then it fades out

A small object
flame-pink

in the middle of the darkness
I can't tell what it is
Different parts are lit up

An object
the color of lava
It shrinks
until it's just an orange dot
in the night

Telephone poles
along a road
along the water

A red, white and blue earth mover
with bright orange blowup tires

A man high above me
on a white path
that snakes upward through plants
with large, dark-green leaves
A garden on a hillside in Europe

A crack in the wall
becomes a
bright blue
jagged window
with a fire
in the middle
It's short-lived

We're all taking a trip somewhere
sailing somewhere

We're sitting high up on a lifeguard's chair

The brightest red parallelogram
inside a bright light blue

A bright light blue
horse
lying on the ground

That is a witch's face
The witch slightly resembles
my onetime friend Melissa Bank
but with a bright orange face
and little white teeth

And now we have the face
of one of our presidents
Teddy Roosevelt or William Howard Taft
with a brushy mustache
and wire-rim glasses
and a glowing bright-red object
floating in the area of his face
Soon there's just the glowing object
and for the life of me
I can't tell what it is
It's like a turd or a snake coiled up
or a weird pretzel
or glow worms
or glowing algae
along the coast

Now a small object
glowing orange
the skeletal head of an animal
with its mouth open
ready to clamp its teeth

A yellow number 1

Two yellow patches
on a park bench
where the sun shines through a tree

Small eyeholes in the gray surface
lit from behind by volcanic red

Small bright red objects
swim in my mind
They swim up
the yellow underwater cliffs

It's early morning or late dusk
The sky is lighter
above a field
in the woods

Driving on a road through reeds and cattails
The car is going too fast on the sweeping curves
It's making me sick to my stomach

July 6, 2011 (later)

▼

Dark snowmen sit there
Dark mountainsides

A dim light in the sky
At the end of the valley

A dark dancer in a purple skirt
Only the skirt is fully visible

Something is trying to enter
At first I thought it was the sun
Later it was more like the moon
But it wasn't either of them

In the dark-green and black world
not a single image emerges
Is this the end of the work?

No, there's a white moth
in the dark maroon air
and orange fish
in the wine-dark sea

I'm lying on the ground
Green light showers
from the top of the sky
The shower of green light
leaves traces all over our bodies

Where are we now?
In foggy tunnels
The fog is flowing toward me
like water

They remind me
of sewer tunnels
But there's nothing
scuzzy
about them

Anything more?
Look for turbulence
There's some in the center
some along the sides
A dark, spiderlike object in the center
But it's all very dark
This is the very first second of dawn

Look through
the small window
along the second flight of stairs
at the formal park
behind the house
It must be a place
I saw in Europe
or in movies
or in novels

A dark maroon space
with white objects in it
eyes
pairs of eyes
women's eyes in a Muslim country

Once again
a valley at night
more than a valley
a bowl
everywhere surrounded by hills

It's hard to see things
A very thin man
in a dark-green shirt
with a thin brown head
against a black background

And these orange
square glass vases
floating in the middle of the black

The eyes of the darkness
have a sorrowful look
The forehead of the darkness
is narrow
and pale

A searchlight moves
horizontally
along the ridge
above the river valley

Why do I keep finding myself
at the latest dusk
or the earliest sunrise?

These are '70s moments
connected with '70s murders

A shark
in the dark tank
partly underlit
by an orange light

Is this a wagon train
walking on a dry Western plain
at late dusk or early dawn
maroon dust in the dark air?

Look, a bright orange object
floats in the black space
directly in front of us
What is it?
Longhorns?
I don't know
Something abstract
A semicircle?
A ring that has been broken open?

Light shines into the black
from behind
and above
a dark green light
But now
the hairy trees
seem to rise up toward the light
and fill the sky
with a hairy blackness

It's one of those times of day again
It's always those times of day
and no people are around
no human things
Perhaps clearings
Clearings are human things
But nothing more
Stages with no props
no actors
almost no light
very little sound
beyond the wind in the trees
very few birds
at this point in the day
if it's the day

A blue light
is shining
on a car
at night
a car driving
along a coast highway
the coast to the left
the coastal hills to the right

We stood and watched the remains
of an orange sunset
above a fence
out West

July 9, 2011

▼

A disfigured face
with a large mouth
wide open
Frankenstein
hovers over the stage

Eagles balance
on fountains

Scum floats
at the stagnant edge
of the ocean

I cross the driveway
to kick the ball
high in the air

A car parked
in the tall weeds
a bit off the road

Please, don't you dare

And what if I see
a movie screen
purple and silver
leaves all coming together?

*

My son, I see a mass shortening
A mass shortening of flowers

A warm light enters the darkness
Blue spots
Thick stars
A bright yellow god
Someone falling upward
like in a Baroque painting

A man in a white bathrobe
getting down from
a horse or camel
Gray stones in the white sun
A white path
into the corn

A miniature ferris wheel

A silver eagle

July 19, 2011

▼

A small deer is feeding
in a field at night

At a dark airport runway
in some far corner of the sky
I wish there were a building
with an office
and a soda machine
and a cigarette machine
and a small bar
the only bar around
in the coastal hamlet
in Scotland or Ireland

I'm looking down into a valley
That's all I can say

The sky is dirty white

We had the choice to live in it once

You wanna make a little less than the operator does

I let my son go much too long ago

A blue fluffy cat sleeps
in one corner of the ceiling

July 21, 2011

▼

A field
in the distance
is partly lit up
by the sun
the only thing in the landscape
the sun lights up

I walk
under an arched
allé of trees
and come out
where there are
tall reeds
and an occasional cedar
along the road
a fancy property ahead
with shapely trees
spaced out in the lawn
and
a person
maybe two people
two women
in long dresses
walking up
toward the house

An earthquake
in slow motion
doesn't appear to do any damage

Beyond an arched metal bridge
over a polluted river
smoke rises
from many smokestacks

A complex
purple metal sculpture
stands
I'm tempted to say
right side up
It seems to be
two figures
hugging each other

July 21, 2011 (late at night)

▼

A spider
in its web
trembles in the wind

We followed the car
through the desert
at night
to a great bonfire

A set of false teeth
sat on the card table
glowing
as if it had a light inside

A stuffed fish
mounted
on a
square piece of wood
glows

A man
with a concerned look on his face
looks for something
on the side of the highway
hot clouds
behind him
What could he be looking for
in the chicory
and queen anne's lace
and poison ivy?

Perhaps a cellphone

A small lake
in the dark backyard

Goalposts
glow in the night
goalposts within goalposts
receding

They gave you no example of this route or that

You see these serial wife abusers
Who say they love too much

The snowman
is now
as tall as the house
It happened accidentally

Why do you think it would be nice to restaurant workers at least once?
Why do you think it would be kosher?

The flame
is only
at the tip of the torch
on top of the trophy

July 22, 2011

▼

A large plowed field
stretches off
toward
a distant valley
infinity

A face
looks at us
through the night
the face
of a race car driver
looking up
at the people around
his low car

The sun
glints
off the steel wheels
of the stopped train

Blue flowers grow
in the black night
They change shape
from circles to squares
to circles to squares

It's night now
The sky is very black
overhead
The sky
is a black
rock
overhead

The sky
is a black cliff
Is the sun
going to rise
from below
our world?

We are lost
among red stars
enveloped by them
We are caught
in a thick web
of red stars
We get wet in it

A small window
in a metal door
at the end
of a long corridor

A beehive
made of
blue sky

The nose cone
of a plane
pokes towards us
It looks like
the brown center
of a black-eyed Susan

Something is there
in the gray space
just beneath
the porch roof

A pink sail
in the night

It's a place where
you're never sure
what you're seeing
Is that a tree
across the road
or something else?
What's it like there
at the base of the trees
in the woods?
There's surprisingly little
underbrush

The pupils
of his eyes
looked like
buttons
As if he were
a doll
or a robot

August 16, 2011

▼

Something pulls me
into the depths of the night
A faint keyhole

A minaret or a steeple
against a blackening
yellow sky

A tiny bat flying
at the bottom
of a gray crater

August 16, 2011 (later)

▼

The world is brown
in danger of catching fire from below

A blue wisp
perhaps a TV screen
in the brown depths

A creature
with a
small
blue head
and big
orange hair
all orange

A flower
with a
darker orange
head
in the middle

What do we want to see
in the shocking blue sky?
What do we want to feel?

*

A pink diagonal being
in the darkness
a fully extended rabbit

A brown profile
in the wan sunlight
just the right amount of sunlight

Something
blue in the night
a blue star
a blue
three-dimensional star
made out of netting
so the air goes through it

An orange skeleton
lives under an orange sky
under an orange and black sky
under a black
and orange sky
under a
black sky

August 20, 2011

▼

It's black out
with a mist of powdered stars

Through the car windshield
a reddish black sky
the end of I don't know what kind of sunset
in I don't know what kind of place

A dim corridor
goes down
and then curves
to the right

A ghostly white canoe
with wheels
glows
in the night

What do we see
when we look
high above us
in a corner
of the throne room?

What did they show us?
It makes you think
they've sold
most of what they have

A gray face
almost emerges
from the center of the black

She is wearing a striking scarf
around her neck
Wouldn't it be great if she were here?
She hates it there

August 20, 2011 (later)

VI

▼

A country road
dips into a lowland
with tall reeds
encroaching
from both sides

July 1, 2012

▼

Everything is very dim

In the maroon post-sunset sky
there seemed to be an island in the distance

An old-fashioned hamburger drive-in where cars pull up to the
    windows
A dark silhouette in a car whose windshield is splashed with light

Deep within the body
in an inner sanctum
a tiny tooth

And look, the battery's running out!

Bubbles on the surface of the water
near the shady bank of the lake

The sun is a fire that flares from below us
The light rises from below
and lights up the things around us

Is that a Native American chieftain
with a tall headdress
running from right to left
in an old movie?

The point where the iceberg
melts
into the ocean
that white and gray
collision

Millard Fillmore, something about Millard Fillmore

There was a very light-blue force on the right
and then it faded, sapped

What do we know about anything?

Again, it's very late in the sunset
or very early in the dawn
out West
in the country

Animal eyes
close up
look at me

July 3, 2012

▼

Stardust is sprinkled
over a black background
A dark shadow spreads
to the center

A piano is tucked in the corner beyond a glass door
like at my sister Alice's house in Pacific Palisades 30 years ago

Look down
the green-ribbed tunnel

The curves
of the chair back
radiate outward
into the space
around them

A thin
Lombardy poplar
or cypress
is reflected in lake water
at night
a fat needle-like line
coming toward me

If there were not more, there would be less

A notch in the mountain range
in the distance
down the dark road

A great chandelier
hanging in a dim room
representing the constellations

An eagle made
of darkened gold
a war medal

A bouquet of sunflowers
that looks like it's etched in silver
in the pitch-black dining room

The monument is finite

I'm on a trail
at night
looking down
into a deep valley
It's a black abyss

Peonies
bloom at night
The black peonies
that bloom at night

July 11, 2012

▼

A blue square glows
in the middle of a white space
and then all fades to black

A black rectangle rises above silver ocean waves

The bells of reindeer tinkle
It must be Christmas time
The ticking of the clock is so relentless
relentless until it stops

A shifting, fuzzy, whitish square
in the middle of the black
A man's face
A demon's face
A cat's face

Go inside
a place very white
white terracotta walls

We start with a white flower
floating on dark water
which the sun
then shines on
and turns bright purple
Then a beach
a curving beach
with a
lagoon
right behind the beach
and people in the lagoon

Then a Cardinal
sitting
Then a man
leaning forward
in a brown robe
yelling out
Then a brick wall
behind the man
which takes over the scene

A woman
a "chemical blonde"
talks animatedly
and then her face
turns into
a pig
and then
some other animal
not a horse

We have a glowing
yellow
frame
around
a pale gray
square
all against
a black background

Now we see a Saudi sheik
Now we see a Christian martyr
with a broad gold halo
almost a Byzantine halo

They decided to cover the world
with wallpaper

blue wallpaper
and its flowery print
is over everything
It's over the whole world

*

Planes
or birds
are swooping in

The sky is yellow
and then orange below that
and then a black horizon

The sky
is a bronze relief

A woman
talking
wearing white clownface
turns into a man
from the era
of Woodrow Wilson
or Teddy Roosevelt
wearing the glasses
of that era
in a sepia photo
He has a stern mien
He has something to tell us

Women are smiling
giant women above me
my mother
my sister

We're not getting through to them

A white face materializes
in the black
an old man
but it never fully comes through
Then it's an animal
a mammal's head
looking up out of a pond
It's like a sheep
but mostly I'm seeing black

July 14, 2012

▼

Grass and weeds
grow up the side of a house
obscuring it
reminding me of a scene
in the original movie of "The Time Machine"

A giant tree
creates
a vast umbrella
over the ground
like one of the trees in "Avatar"

He has a giant penis
and thin wings
maybe more than two wings

I don't know if that's correcting science or mixed
I just don't know

Sorrow doesn't insist
It must be done like this

Here's the bright blue square again
with the white frame

A white circular blob
against black
A yellow frond above

We'll see by then

Lawyers who are most vital are leaving with the Lees

Once the swinger in front of you leaves

July 15, 2012

▼

Look
a powdery green light
turns black
and then
a giant
bowman
with the biggest bow
made of blond wood

Look
a purple square
inside
a light gray square
and then
black all around
Look
a round white mist
in the center
that could
become a head
but doesn't

You ever call us that
a man's voice threatens

Look
dark green depths

Look
a man holds his little daughter's hand
She doesn't reach his waist yet

July 20, 2012

▼

A man and a child
Then nothing
for a long time nothing

What about now?
Just a starry night

Seated girls
clapping their hands

July 25, 2012

▼

An overstuffed brown couch
against a darker brown wall
a small yellow window
high up on the right

See, that is a painting
a brown couch against a brown wall
a small yellow window
That is a painting
the beginning of a whole oeuvre of paintings

These agreements tire us
Our agreements tire us

So they got him before they called him up

I'm not sure what I'm seeing now
in this pea-soup atmosphere
but it makes me feel very sympathetic
to someone there

The ocean through skinny palm trunks
an image from Hawaii

A blonde woman getting off a bus
with a long thick braid running down her back
and large brown sunglasses

Why?
They better not say them

A bougainvillea bush conceals a doorway
It's my niece Abby's house in Los Angeles

July 29, 2012

▼

At the end
of a long corridor
a door
with a small window
and dusty light
shining out

July 30, 2012

▼

A chin-up bar
glows orange
in the darkness

The road
curves
to the left
at night

I looked at a tree
and it seemed to flex its muscles
The tree flexed its muscles

I must be floating
downstream
toward a lit bridge
at night
in a city
The lit bridge
is reflected
on the water
ahead

A giant bird
as big as a house
puts its beak
against a large window
and looks inside

That didn't put an end to the war
It shouldn't have

The guy at the bowling alley says, 'Who will stand to pick?'

It's not gonna cure that ID problem
We're gonna head out into the room

I see water outside the picture window
In the distance
a dark peninsula
with a hill
not unlike Schoodic Head in Maine

I'm looking into a movie projector
It's showing a movie about Abe Lincoln
but way too bright
everything bleached by sun

That's a lot of agents for 10 months

An empty ballfield at night
a big place at night

We'll figure out a goal this time

Again, a bridge over a river
but this time it's a footbridge
I'm thinking of walking over the footbridge
instead of floating across the river in a ferry

An electrified
white picket fence
pulses orange
at night

Well, that depends on what he does

A long low motel
brown with yellow trim
a couple of windows

on the small second floor
where the roof
is decoratively triangulated

A cat sits in a litter box
Two cats sit in a litter box

July 31, 2012

▼

I see a woman
with short dirty blonde hair
who looks like
Martina Navratilova

A bamboo thicket at night
Nothing threatening about it

I almost see something over there
to the right
a field
behind
a stone wall
some yellow
wildflowers

You don't need to be in graduate school to do that

I'm seeing that square again
It's a dim square
milky white
and it quickly becomes
a milky white circle
a vague circle
on the way to becoming a face

Well, things have been hard for you once or twice

You're letting the tires go
That's a silver play
You're seeing your friends

Fairness to you guys that you have to stay there

I thought you had to go to Mexico

What do we see here?
...which is to keep the net

People like us
We have to have three baths

Remember the explorers union
Inheritance
On your side
That's what we're trying to do

August 2, 2012

VII

▼

There are two places to go
for the steamboat.
Look, there's this whole space
beneath the steamboat.

It had snowed.
There was no place to find out.

A car is driving away
on a curving road.
First it curves to the right
and then it curves to the left
out of sight.

A Buddhist leader
is standing off to the right
in a red robe
with a kind of Mohawk,
a complex pattern
of hair
and shaved head.
He walked to the left
and turned into a woman.

Walk through the white rooms
of an empty gallery
with an unpainted wooden floor
and take a left
into a kind of corridor
behind the biggest room
and then that corridor jogs to the right.

One thing to ask you
You weren't disappointed in this job?

July 8, 2013

▼

We pass a big sign—
NO VICIOUS BONE—
for an outdoor rock concert.

A brown slat fence
curving to the left
along with the road.

A yellow day lily
grows from the back right tire
of a VW Beetle
parked in the weeds.

Beyond, a green field
with small yellow flowers.

July 9, 2013

▼

A yellow construction vehicle
forced me to slow down
on a country road.
I swung around it on the left
and back into the lane.
It was right after that
a blue sports car shot out
from a little road on the right.

July 10, 2013

ACKNOWLEDGMENTS

Close Your Eyes was first published in 2018 as an ebook by Argotist Online in the U.K. Previously, 15 of its prose poems were published as a chapbook exchanged with members of the Dusie Kollektiv in Zurich in 2013, and 11 were published in the ezines *Drunken Boat* and *Horse Less Review* and the print magazine *Enchanted Verses Literary Review*.

Twenty-four poems from *Visions* were first published in the ezines *Otoliths*, *BlazeVOX*, *First Literary Review-East*, *Unlikely Stories*, *SurVision* and *Noon: journal of the short poem*, in the print magazine *The Hurricane Review* and in the *ANYDSWPE 2021 Anthology*.

Thanks to Jeffrey Side of Argotist Online, Susana Gardner and the late Marthe Reed of the Dusie Kollektiv and the editors of the other publications.

Thanks to the late Bernadette Mayer, Delia Ungureanu, George Quasha, Matvei Yankelevich, Nancy Graham, Owen Andrews, Peter Baker and Sam Truitt for their poetic advice.

Michael Handler Ruby is a poet, literary editor and journalist. He is the author of seven other full-length poetry collections, including *At an Intersection* (Alef Books, 2002), *Window on the City* (BlazeVOX [books], 2006), *The Edge of the Underworld* (BlazeVOX, 2010), *Compulsive Words* (BlazeVOX, 2010), *American Songbook* (Ugly Duckling Presse, 2013), *The Mouth of the Bay* (BlazeVOX, 2019) and *The Star-Spangled Banner* (Station Hill Press, 2020). His trilogy in prose and poetry, *Memories, Dreams and Inner Voices* (Station Hill, 2012), includes the e-books *Fleeting Memories* (Ugly Duckling, 2008) and *Inner Voices Heard Before Sleep* (Argotist Online, 2011). He is also the author of the ebook *Titles & First Lines* (Mudlark, 2018) and five chapbooks with the Dusie Kollektiv. He co-edited Bernadette Mayer's collected early books, *Eating the Colors of a Lineup of Words* (Station Hill, 2015), and Mayer's and Lewis Warsh's prose collaboration *Piece of Cake* (Station Hill, 2020). A graduate of Harvard College and Brown University's writing program, he grew up in South Orange, N.J., and lives in Brooklyn.